Seize the Cloud

A Manager's Guide to Success
with Cloud Computing

Erik van Ommeren • Sogeti USA
Martin van den Berg • Sogeti Netherlands

With:
Jean-Michel **Bertheaud** • IBM France
Per **Björkegren** • Sogeti Sweden
Rik **den Boogert** • Sogeti Netherlands
Flavien **Boucher** • Sogeti France
Bernard **Huc** • Sogeti France
Daniël **Jumelet** • Sogeti Netherlands
Mark **Kerr** • IBM UK
Alfonso **Lopez de Arenosa** • Sogeti Spain
Eric **Michiels** • IBM Belgium
Ron **Moerman** • Sogeti Netherlands
Brian **Naylor** • IBM UK
Bert **Noorman** • Sogeti Netherlands
Liam **Ó Móráin** • Data Fonics Germany
Paul **Poelmans** • Sogeti Belgium
Ewald **Roodenrijs** • Sogeti Netherlands
Pascal **Sire** • IBM France
Jimmy **Sterner** • Sogeti Sweden
Sunil **Talreja** • Sogeti USA

2011
IBM and Sogeti

©2011   IBM and Sogeti

production	LINE UP boek en media bv, Groningen, the Netherlands
design	Jan Faber
editing	Susan MacFarlane
final editing	Minke Sikkema
cover photo	Sunsine and Shadow Arch (www.flickr.com > Ross2085)
ISBN	978-90-75414-32-5

Contents

Acclaim for Seize the Cloud

The writers have managed to create a well-structured and easy-to-read book, the biggest challenge for anyone writing a book about a hype thing like cloud. The most important benefit from the book is that it creates an understanding and definition of cloud from a business perspective. The book has well-described and interesting practical cases, which in combination with the theory gives me the foundation for crafting our future cloud strategy.

Göran Bengtsson
CIO Öresundskraft AB (Sweden)

For hype-weary IT and business management, this book will be a breath of fresh air. We all know that cloud is the future of commoditized IT (not all IT), but how do we get there, and how do we make sure it all hangs together? The worst thing any manager could do is listen to the industry hype that once again promises a new IT utopia. This book deals with the real issues and offers a mature roadmap for cloud adoption—no organization should embark on a cloud strategy without it.

Martin Butler
Founder of Martin Butler Research

Developing an emerging-technology strategy requires coordination across IT; like any strategic IT activity, it has an impact on relationship management, architecture, delivery, operations, and support. It's not just about technology selection but also about IT's ability to operate IT as a collection of business services—sourced from internal and external clouds. This book speaks to this concept.

Bobby Cameron
Vice President, Principal Analyst, Forrester Research Inc.

In this book Erik van Ommeren and Martin van den Berg break out the most important concept of cloud computing, how it works within your enterprise and how to plan for it. I would recommend this book to anyone who needs to both understand cloud, and define a strategy.

David Linthicum
CTO Blue Mountain Labs

Yankee Group's research points to the maturation of our global network into the pervasive, intelligent fabric that businesses need to support cloud-based computing, allowing them to evolve to Anywhere Enterprises. This book, rich with all the ambition associated with this exciting new model, but threaded with real-world stories, tough questions, and pragmatic advice, is an essential guide for business leaders tackling the next great computing revolution. Don't leave home without it.

Emily Nagle Green
Chairman, Yankee Group Research, and author, Anywhere

This book will help considerably. For sure, it contains all the definitions, insights and perspectives that get a firm grip on the cloud phenomenon. It's *all the bible you need*, if you like. But more importantly, it is down-to-earth, pragmatic and action-oriented. This is illustrated by many cases from real life, telling us about inspiring people and their businesses, already exploring, testing, learning and benefiting from the cloud.
Exactly what is needed to put the rubber on the road. Stop evangelizing, start reading. Then act.

Ron Tolido
CTO Applications Continental Europe, Capgemini
Director, The Open Group

Foreword by IBM

During my more than 30 years in the technology industry, I have been fortunate to have played an active role in shaping the innovations that have revolutionized the way technology impacts business. Cloud computing is one of those innovations. Much more than a way to save on technology costs by sharing computing resources, cloud computing has a profound impact on all types of institutions from business to education, government and health care.

What makes cloud computing so powerful is that it breaks down barriers between silo and proprietary applications, both inside and outside an organization. For the first time, the entire ecosystem can freely share information and ideas. New partnerships and ways of thinking will undoubtedly emerge as students on opposite ends of the world learn together, large and small governments work together and employees and clients create together.

Cloud computing also makes enterprises smarter by delivering analytics capabilities that they never had before. With this, businesses can turn their raw data into valuable information that provides insight and predicts outcomes. This level of reliable information enables organizations to make better, more accurate business decisions.

Built on the wisdom of services-oriented architecture, cloud computing further accelerates agility and flexibility. Since businesses can tap into resources beyond what they own, they can respond more quickly to business needs and changing conditions. IT departments can better balance their costs, risks and time-to-delivery.

Cloud computing is not a new buzzword. Its foundation has existed for years and it will continue to set the pace for how technology will be used, consumed and delivered, long into the future. As you read through this book, you will come to more fully understand the impact and implications of cloud computing for your enterprise and see it as a way to leverage technology to make your business a leader.

Steve Mills
Senior Vice President and Group Executive
IBM Software and Systems

Foreword by Sogeti

Using computing power in the same way we use electricity? It makes so much sense, doesn't it. When you need it, you turn it on, and when you don't need it anymore, you turn it off. You only pay for the power you actually use, without having to worry about sudden peaks in demand or huge upfront investment in hardware and software. Computing should have been set up as a utility in the first place. It should have been a no-brainer to implement it. And why stop there, at the hardware level? Why not set up a similar service for storage, network connectivity or even software applications? It would certainly take away a lot of unwanted complexity and create tremendous possibilities for efficiencies.

This is—in a nutshell—the thought behind cloud computing, and explains much of the deafening hype that is going on around this new computing model. However, it is important to realize that cloud computing in its essence is not new. Already in 1963 there was talk about utility-style computing, and since then the concept has surfaced in many forms only to disappear again under the waves of technological progress. Although the concept has always been clear, all the necessary elements to make cloud computing a mainstream success were simply not available.

But this time around it is different. Bringing together many innovations, cloud computing and cloud services have gained mainstream popularity in the consumer space and are now quickly spreading into the enterprise world. Sharing and storing huge amounts of photos online has become the norm, solving challenges around security and reliability in a much better way than an individual ever could. Making a video available to the world no longer requires a broadcast network; it is done using a readily available service that is (so far) offered for free. And email has truly become a commodity that is consumed by the millions through an online service that is financed completely through advertising.

However promising cloud computing might seem, we have to realize that complexity hardly ever disappears. It cannot be reduced, only hidden. This simple fact should be printed as a disclaimer on the "wrappers" of every cloud offering and service. Yes, cloud computing is "oversold" by overly enthusiastic optimistic suppliers, but is also "overbought" by people who (want to) believe that simple solutions to complex problems do exist.

This book describes how the concept of utility computing has been brewing and maturing in small advances that now add up to the cloud revolution. It discusses the vast opportunities that come with this fourth model for computing after the mainframe, client/server and the web. It describes the continuing trend of virtualization of technology in support of business and looks at how this trend will eventually start to virtualize business processes in the not too distant future. But what the book also does is explain that nothing comes for free. Cloud computing involves trade-offs that are too important to leave up to the technologists. The owners of business processes will need to get involved to make the most out of this new wave. The authors make the case for embracing cloud computing as more than a technology change. It describes that, especially for a CIO or enterprise architect, the changes on the horizon are promising and exciting, but at the same time can be daunting. Will you lose control or finally become part of the innovation cycle of your organization? (As you will find out, the answer to that question is "a bit of both".)

I would like to invite you to read this book, use it to craft your strategy and engage with the authors directly to continue the conversation, to look at cloud in the context of your organization and to deepen our mutual understanding of what this next revolution will mean to 21st century business.

Michiel Boreel
Chief Technology Officer
Sogeti

1   The New Business Reality

If you are an IT decision maker, then cloud computing will change your role and your relevance to your organization, but in ways that you probably don't expect. By too many, cloud is still perceived as an IT infrastructural matter that is best left to the technicians. This observation was one of the important reasons for writing this book. Cloud must be used as a much more strategic opportunity, and right now is the best time to start doing so. In your organization, you can now position cloud computing in such a way that it will help you outcompete and outperform your competitors. Your active role in this transformation will be crucial and personally rewarding.

You probably know how cloud can help you lower cost, reduce overhead capacity and how that will make you achieve your ever present cost-cutting goals. You may even be thinking about using cloud computing to improve "agility" and time to market: faster response to business demands. But that's not it. That is not the big impact of cloud. These are undoubtedly great goals to pursue, and cloud will help you achieve them. But in a couple of years we'll have seen a much bigger impact of cloud; an impact that transforms the business reality.

A time of transformation

In today's business environment, it seems that unpredictability and highly dynamic markets have become the norm. In their book *Chaotics*, Philip Kotler and John Caslione (Kotler and Caslione 2009) state that the world of commerce and business is in a state of transition and will never be the same again. The latest recession marked a clear paradigm shift. The economy is moving from a pattern of predictable cycles of prosperity and recession into a much more turbulent world where highs and lows appear with greater frequency, which is to some extent an effect of ongoing globalization. This has become the new world of business: international, connected and chaotic.

In this context, cloud computing is not simply changing the way we do technology; it is changing the way we do business. In much the same way that social media has completely changed marketing, advertising and even news and public opinion, cloud computing is changing business, changing products and services, changing markets and even changing innovation itself.

It's hard to overemphasize the potential effect of the transformation to cloud computing. Nicholas Carr is quoted everywhere in this regard. He wrote the book *The Big Switch* (Carr 2009). In this book he predicts that in the coming decade or so corporate IT will be more or less "switched off" in favor of cloud resources. In this scenario, the time and attention currently required to maintain the commodity components of your business would decrease dramatically. You could start to focus on what creates real value for the organization: the innovation process (and culture) itself, where technology is no longer a barrier.

From product to service

Another effect of cloud computing is that the *products* we use and create turn into *services*. Here a new vendor-client relationship comes into view: one based on continuity, recurrence and trust. Just try to sell a service that doesn't do what you promise: the client will simply stop using it. We also talk about services in a different way than we talk about products: services are generally marketed in terms of *what they do* rather than *what they are*: we make the decision at a higher level of abstraction. In reality, this move to cloud computing will result in a more dynamic set of partners that will need to be *managed*, or better, kept engaged. And the services you use will become an integral part of the services you offer to your own clients. The shared responsibility demands shared goals, shared risks and shared benefits. This introduces a new kind of market where pricing can continually fluctuate, and price may be based less on the *size* of a solution and more on the *value* provided and how many competing offerings there are to choose from. In this market, an IT manager could become something similar to a corporate venture capitalist.

A corporate venture capitalist
When we view IT as a business, it may be managed in the model of a venture capitalist striving for the best return on investment while at the same time exploiting market opportunities. Cloud computing makes it possible to invest in a vast set of business solutions (services) and rely on the law of averages, which says it's better to invest in a broad series of initiatives than to pour all the capital into one. The returns on those

initiatives that prove successful are more than enough to pay for the losses on those initiatives that fail.

The overall return on invested capital will surpass the expected return from traditional, slower and less broad business solution development.

Another investment approach that cloud computing makes possible is a bootstrap approach: a small initial investment may get your business going, then reinvesting the profits from each sale will enable you to grow your business. Especially for smaller companies, this approach can be very attractive.

With technology and processes already spreading inside and outside the organization, we've reached a point where truly we need to start *thinking in systems of systems*. And since every business activity is taking place in this connected ecosystem, we need to rethink our business concept itself. *We need to start thinking in businesses built from other businesses.*

Seen in this light, it is clear that cloud computing is not a goal in itself: it enables your company to be part of the ecosystem. Clearly, you cannot afford to ignore cloud computing. In an ecosystem of connected companies, the ones that do not participate cannot win. If your systems are not suited for transactional interaction, you will not get the business. If your organization is not capable of maintaining good service relationships (keeping your partners and customers happy enough to stay with you), then you will lose your market share.

When your company is part of this ecosystem, it is not a one-way street. You could just as easily become a service provider instead of only being a service consumer. You can open up parts of your business to the partners in your ecosystem: if you have data that is attractive to others or if you have unique expertise in performing certain calculations, you could make these available through commercially viable services and extend your business.

Business technology

Finally there is the impact of technology on *the business* itself. With tech-savvy users, clients and management, business decisions are increasingly becoming technology decisions. Many business processes are so technologically enhanced that we are in fact running Cyborg businesses: business and technology are interwoven. We have moved from information technology to business technology. Technological innovation and business innovation are synonymous, and technology brings direct business opportunities. And there are lots of opportunities here: at the moment there are many innovations available that have not yet been fully embraced by organizations or society. We have yet to realize the opportunities they present.

It may sound a bit far-fetched or futuristic, but most of this is happening today: people and companies are becoming smarter in using technology. Marketing technologies, for example, are almost completely in the hands of the business decision-makers, not IT (Woods 2010). There are even companies who have no internal IT anymore. It does not make business sense to fight this inevitable shift; your company size, industry or even how innovative you are today cannot keep you immune from this change.

Where cloud computing can contribute to business innovation

Some examples:

- Compete in a global "low price" market, with high volume and low margin.
- Speed up innovation by engaging customers and partners, and be the first to market a hot item.
- Monetize all parts of your business. Any system, resource or process that is valuable for someone else can be sold as a service (B2B or B2C).
- Monetize your data. Turn existing data into usable information and identify new business opportunities for yourself or sell the information to others.
- Simplify the on-boarding of new customers. Use a payment structure that attracts new customers, for example through free trials and free services that can be upgraded.
- Win in "turns." Increase responsiveness to quickly adapt in downturns (and upturns) to get ahead of the competition.

The roles of CIO and IT

In recent years, the role of the CIO has been a subject of much discussion. About how he could be an innovator or a catalyst for change. In reality, not much of that has materialized: most often the CIO is still perceived as the person keeping IT in order while trying to reduce costs. This will not change overnight. The most realistic scenario is a slow shift towards the innovator role, which would ultimately be rewarding both for the company (since technological innovation is business innovation) and for the CIO personally (expanding opportunities rather than just operations).

Now is the perfect time to start that shift. There is still time to develop an IT department that is trained and ready for its new role, that adapts quickly with the business side and becomes a department famous for saying "Yes" instead of saying "No." Then replace whatever makes sense with a cloud alternative, and aggressively start connecting with others.

The most important focus from the start must be a process oriented one. Create the right processes that enable quick responses while preventing future spaghetti resulting from a series of quick solutions. Design your governance and enterprise architecture not from the perspective of risk management, but from the perspective of enabling best-in-class customer service. Keep it lightweight and dynamic. Start comparing yourself to external service providers and make sure that you win the comparison every time. In simple terms, start applying what you know already. You may cautiously want to wait, thinking there will be a better time, but that is false hope. There is no reason to wait. The world will not become less volatile. Budget pressures will remain and technology will keep on evolving. The sooner you start experimenting, the sooner you will climb the learning curve and develop a full appreciation of how cloud computing will change your business, your role and your future.

Reading guide

The rest of this book will introduce you to everything you need to get started. "Chapter 2: A Dozen Bold Statements on Cloud Computing" will give you more food for thought, while covering the basic concepts of cloud computing. "Chapter 3: Business Innovation Through Cloud Computing" will make the case for embracing business technology and the effect it has on IT as we know it. Then we will dive into the economic model, describing the parties and interactions of cloud computing in "Chapter 4: Cloud Economics," followed by how business and IT work together and the impact of cloud computing on the internal IT department in "Chapter 5: The New IT Constitution."

Since integration and reducing enterprise risk will be essential in anything related to cloud, "Chapter 6: Enterprise Architecture for Cloud's Sake" details how enterprise architecture plays a role, and how you can employ it while remaining pragmatic and nimble. "Chapter 7: Overcoming the Barriers" will put some supposed barriers in perspective and counter any unrealistic hype or negativity that may still surround cloud.

"Chapter 8: Data: The New Frontier" is giving you insight into the question of what happens next, when cloud is omnipresent and data is more openly shared. And finally "Chapter 9: Creating Your Roadmap" will help you put together your own journey to the cloud, with some concrete steps and pointers on how to advance.

In between these chapters you will find case studies based on interviews with CIO's from companies that have started to embrace cloud computing. In these tales of the real experiences of a wide range of companies, you will read how they solved their issues, found value, and became satisfied (or not) with cloud. With this combination of vision, approach and real-life experiences, we give you a strong foundation for seizing the opportunity that is the cloud.

Shell International Doing Groundwork to Create Pure Cloud Computing Model
Cloud to Serve as Default Environment for IT Services Going Forward

When it comes to cloud computing, Shell International B.V. is moving full steam ahead. With contracts already in place to integrate cloud services from Microsoft and Amazon Web Services with its own internal IT service environment, Shell's strategy is clear: Anything that can run in the cloud should, in fact, do just that.

Except for the mission-critical applications with the greatest availability requirements and most sensitive data, everything is a candidate. "The cloud is default," says Johan Krebbers, VP of architecture and group IT architect.

If that strategy sounds cavalier, it's only because in Krebbers' view, the cloud is nothing special. Rather, it's a natural step in the evolution of IT and should be considered an important tool that carries with it the same requirements—creating, maintaining, provisioning and managing—that are normally associated with more traditional IT resources. And for users, it should be completely transparent.

The goal, says Krebbers, is to create a hybrid environment of public cloud applications and traditional IT services, running on an infrastructure-as-a-service (Amazon's Elastic Compute Cloud) and accessible via a single-sign-on, Web-based interface. To date, deployed cloud services have been limited to specific production environments, such as SharePoint development, while the company has availed itself to one-off software-as-a-service offerings such as Salesforce.com. Eventually, however, users will access everything they need from that unified interface.

"For a business user it is a complete black box whether a service at the end is delivered by the internal IT department, one of the traditional infrastructure service providers or one of the cloud providers," Krebbers says.

The Road to Flexibility Does Not Go Through Traditional IT

Like many companies experimenting with cloud computing, Shell sees the cloud as a path to new levels of business agility as the company becomes increasingly able to deploy services much more quickly—services that offer added flexibility in comparison with the applications they replace. But Shell also sees benefits in offering its employees business versions of the kinds of tools that are already available to consumers—things such as web-based email and social networking.

What Shell is not interested in doing is either establishing its own cloud-enabled data center, or turning to one of the big IT services firms to host its service environment. Krebbers says those options—favored by many companies that aren't comfortable with the perceived risks of true cloud computing—simply can't deliver the flexibility and infinite capacity that cloud providers can, and at a much lower cost.

"The private cloud is nonsense since some critical cloud components cannot be delivered here," says Krebbers. "Cloud providers are much more flexible than traditional IT service providers."

Company Kicking the Tires to Ensure Readiness of Cloud Strategy

Before Shell can achieve its cloud vision, however, it is being careful to mitigate any potential risks. It's performing tests in the areas of high performance computing and storage to determine the extent to which the cloud can be tapped for both. Additionally, as part of its contracts with Amazon and Microsoft, the company has access to SAS 70 audit results (as performed by an external auditor) to ensure that both vendors have the adequate controls and safeguards needed to protect their customers' data and services.

Shell also has set up a cloud computing Centre of Excellence with one of its key suppliers to cope with cloud-related challenges, such as how to handle issues such as security, active directory and application housekeeping. Through the centre, Shell and its supplier will work together to develop standards, support cloud projects and manage the creation and delivery of services.

It may sound as if Shell is going to great lengths to make sure it's on the right path, cloud-wise, and that's with good reason. The company envisions the cloud giving it the ability to deliver more flexible services to business users in the most convenient possible way, rendering them as internal services made available across the organization with a single interface.

It's a grand vision—and one that warrants the ground work Shell is doing to ensure that it progresses as planned.

Hyatt Hotels' Traditional Approach to the Cloud Delivering Business Agility
Hotelier's Journey Started with Long-Ago Decision to Outsource IT

Hyatt Hotels Corp. hasn't had to make the decision to jump into cloud computing—it's been journeying into the cloud since long before anyone was calling it that.

For all intents and purposes, Hyatt began its cloud journey 16 years ago, when the company outsourced the bulk of its IT staff, eventually entrusting the hosting of its primary reservations system to the same IT outsourcer. What's known today as cloud computing was still a long way off, but those moves established an IT philosophy that has become the foundation of Hyatt's cloud strategy.

"We don't want to be in the information technology business," says CIO Mike Blake. "So what we do is get people who can manage our information technology needs."

That's why all these years later, Hyatt's legacy reservations system is still hosted by the same IT outsourcer. By the end of the year, Hyatt will have a backup to that system running in a German data center run by Amadeus, which hosts one of the travel industry's huge booking platforms, known as a "global distribution system." Hyatt's reservation system is one of just two legacy components remaining in the company, the other being a group sales tool, which is also hosted, and for which Blake says there is simply not an alternative on the market, cloud or not.

Cloud Strategy Driven by Desire for Reliable Network

Outside of those legacy systems, Hyatt operates with an increasingly modern cloud computing mindset. With an IT staff of just 43 people supporting a global hospitality company that employs tens of thousands of people at nearly 450 properties worldwide, it's no wonder that just about every application Hyatt runs has been Internet-enabled.

Most notably, the company's Micros property management, Oracle financials and PeopleSoft HR systems are hosted by providers such as Navisite and AT&T, with all of them rendered as Web-based software-as-a-service applications. Hyatt opted to put best-of-breed applications in the hands of those big names to tap their robust and reliable networks, rather than turning to niche SaaS vendors and relying on the vagaries of the public Internet.

"So often, we take the network for granted," says Blake. "You need to make sure your speeds are appropriate, because latency is inexcusable. People get very upset when apps are rendered offsite and they're slower."

Hyatt Uses Old-School Negotiation Strategies for Cloud Procurement

Despite its penchant for traditional hosting arrangements, Hyatt is experimenting with more nimble cloud technologies, as well. For instance, the company is tapping the on-demand computing power of Amazon Web Services' Elastic Compute Cloud to quickly establish development environments for new Web sites that then are managed with a recently deployed content management system residing on servers hosted by AT&T. The content management system is used only as a Web-based interface for quickly making changes to Hyatt's several hundred Web sites, but that limited functionality is having a big impact, with changes that used to take weeks now being completed in minutes.

Given Hyatt's history, it should come as no surprise that the advent of cloud computing offerings like EC2 hasn't changed the strategic discussion of how to manage the company's IT. In fact, Hyatt has come at cloud computing with a decidedly old-school approach to negotiating, working out deals that Blake says ensure that prices fall over time, rather than rising with inflation, which is often how cloud providers structure their deals.

That negotiating strength is a direct reflection of Blake's background as an expert in IT finance. In fact, Blake believes that deal-making is evolving into the skill most required of modern CIOs.

"You want the person who can understand what you need from the cloud and be able to structure a deal such that you got the best rate, not only now, but in the future," says Blake. "At the end of the day, it's procurement and vendor management that becomes a core competency and a differentiator."

CIO Characterizes Hosting-Intensive Model as "Cloud Cheating"

To some, it may sound like a stretch to call much of what Hyatt is doing "cloud computing," and even Blake admits that what Hyatt is doing is "cloud cheating." The way he sees it, users don't care how an application is rendered; rather, they simply want to be able to put data to use in the most convenient way possible, and as quickly as possible. In that sense, ensuring the performance and reliability of the network can become more important than the way applications are rendered.

"I don't have to go to an explicit cloud provider to be in the cloud," he says. "Anyone can have a warehouse and a box, throw a T-1 in there and call themselves the cloud."

What matters most to Blake is how Hyatt uses the data its applications generate. Whether that data comes from a hosted application or a pure SaaS offering is of little issue, so long as the company can put that data to use quickly and efficiently. Today, Hyatt's ability to make the most of its data has made it as nimble as a big company can hope to be, and it has the cloud in its various forms to thank for that.

"If you had a house with multiple rooms in it and you wanted to be a hotel, all you need is a browser, and I can make you a Hyatt Hotel," says Blake. "It's an extremely powerful place to be."

2 A Dozen Bold Statements on Cloud Computing

2.1 Introduction

Today information technology is at a crossroads once again. With every innovation, including the introduction of the first computer, companies have had to choose: adopt now, get ready to adopt, or just wait and see. Cloud computing presents a similar choice: embrace the new concepts, or stick to the old. But cloud computing is different. It's not a new technology or new device, but a new way of using the technology and devices. It's a different model, which requires an analysis at a higher level. It makes us ask how should we do IT, and fundamentally, how should we do business? This chapter will highlight some important aspects of cloud computing and along the way we introduce all the basic concepts that make up cloud computing.

Although there is not a single authority that can exactly define and prescribe what cloud computing is, it is helpful to have a common starting point. The following definition by Forrester Research is particularly helpful. It contains all the elements commonly associated with cloud computing:

> Cloud computing: *"A standardized IT capability (services, software or infrastructure) delivered via Internet technologies in a pay-per-use, self-service way"* (Ried 2010)

The only key element that is not directly addressed in this definition is the scalability or elasticity that cloud computing is supposed to provide. It is indirectly included in the "self service" and "pay-per-use" characteristics. Perhaps a more complete definition would say that ideal or "perfect" cloud computing is "A standardized, *often highly elastic*, IT capability..." Ultimately, it's not debating the definition that creates value; it's finding out how you can use the different models available for your organization's benefit. So let's see what this new development can bring to your organization.

2.2   The Economy Created the Cloud

When the Internet (or more precisely, the World Wide Web) reached critical mass, it wasn't one single technological innovation that made it possible. It was the combination of many separate trends and elements that, when put together, created something that had the enormous potential we see online today. The components (for example, communications protocols, hypertext with hyperlinks, and a domain-naming convention and architecture) were all available and valuable in themselves, but it was the combination that created the Internet. The introduction of the web browser Mosaic is generally considered the final push that truly launched the web.

A similar thing is happening with cloud computing. The term "cloud computing" is one in a long line of other terms and acronyms, all indicating more or less similar developments that create new levels of abstraction, loosening the bonds between process, software code and hardware. "On-demand," "grid computing," "software-as-a service" (SaaS), but also "service-oriented architecture" (SOA) and even "object orientation" (OO) were all terms marking our progress towards ever more flexible and descriptive forms of IT. If you pick apart the elements that make up the current trends, many concepts were available in earlier incarnations. Any definition of cloud computing could easily be applied to a combination of prior similar themes.

Forrester Research mentions three major trends that, combined and in the context of the economic downturn, gave birth to cloud computing (Matzke 2010):
1. Industrialized IT, through increased commoditization, standardization, consolidation and globalization.
2. Tech Populism, a popular culture where technology is consumed by and focused on end consumers, and is no longer the exclusive terrain of organizational buyers.
3. Technology that is embodied in the business, or *business technology* instead of information technology.

Industrialization in IT
Throughout the years, IT has been moving away from the one-off manual processes to a more mature, scientific and automated approach. Examples of this increased maturity are these long-running themes that are evident in cloud computing:

- Thinking about layers and abstractions in software. Object orientation, components, service-oriented architecture, all try to hide the technology as much as possible and find a level of abstraction that is both relevant and stable over time. The emergence of all kinds of standards is an important part of this development.
- Looking for parts of the business or technology that have in fact become a commodity. From the outside in, organizations have been trying to save money by moving away from customized or custom-made software in favor of "commercial-off-the-shelf" (COTS) or dedicated service providers for any process or component that is not adding competitive value.
- Increasing hardware virtualization. In the past few years, the virtualization solutions gained maturity, and using them promised a quick way to save money or hardware by using virtual machines on top of a more or less integrated hardware platform. A direct result of thinking in abstractions applied to hardware itself.

A question comes to mind: what triggered the hype? If many of these concepts were already there, why is cloud computing taking off now? One explanation is that the hype has been brewing for at least a decade under names such as SaaS or ASP (application service provisioning), so it was inevitable that after the SOA hype, SaaS and then cloud computing would follow. Another explanation is that some important software components have now become available or stable enough to be used for core business processes. Most notably, virtualization software has advanced greatly in recent years. The final trigger may have come from the increasingly self-service approach to provisioning IT, an approach that we all know from our personal experiences online.

But what truly pushed cloud computing into the limelight were the economic pressures on IT to save money, become more agile and "find a better way" of doing IT altogether. The trend in IT has been that maintenance costs have kept on rising year over year, consuming an ever-increasing share of the total IT costs and leaving hardly any budget for business innovation. This trend could not continue.

To quote a recent blog post on the topic, "Managing IT is expensive, way too complicated and rarely a core business function that differentiates most companies. But throw in virtualization software, secure multi-tenancy and the proliferation of broadband networks—all technologies that weren't available until recently—then layer on a heavy dose of economic recession, and cloud computing becomes not only possible, but very attractive" (Maitland 2009).

2.3   Cloud Represents All That is Good in IT

Many variations of cloud computing exist, and probably there are cloud implementations that do not neatly fit any definition. So why call it all cloud computing? Some variations may not be standardized, some are not scalable and others are not self-provisioned. Perhaps the one most common denominator in all manifestations of cloud computing is the distinction between ownership versus usage of IT assets. Not everything that is used is automatically owned. Cloud products and services make the sharing of IT assets across projects, applications or even companies economically and operationally viable.

Changing the ownership of the IT assets brings important advantages. The provider can specialize and thereby create an economy of scale. The provider can then promise specialized services, lower price, better performance, higher reliability, more agility, shorter time to market and better quality. Emergence of multiple providers can create a competitive market, which should improve service and reduce prices. At the same time, when the provider is external to the organization, it also introduces the major complexities that are associated with cloud computing:
- How to guarantee security and reliability ("can I trust the provider?").
- How to integrate the external and internal assets into one usable solution.

Most external cloud providers today try to optimize on speed of provisioning and low cost, which leads to commoditized and highly standardized services: one size fits all (with sometimes limited configurability). This is not inherent in the model: providers could very well choose to create much more customized services that take longer to provision. Some smaller, local providers are following this path, while large global players stick to the highly standardized offerings. A local provider may, for example, offer any specific version of an operating system in their cloud, while Amazon or Azure would give you just one, or a limited choice.

When it comes to paying for the use of services, a pay-per-use model sounds ideal: you only pay for what you use. On the other hand, it may be very unpredictable, and for budgeting reasons you might prefer a one-time-fee that covers all. Additionally, pay-per-use can mean many different things. Is that pay per user? Or per click? Per server? Per transaction? Per dollar of goods sold? Some argue that costs should be related to the business revenue, but very few service providers are ready to offer a contract that makes the price completely dependent on the revenue stream as generated by the user. And while the concept of pay-per-use is certainly part of the cloud theme, it is by no means exclusively tied to it: remember the ASP's or even mainframe service bureaus?

Does all that mean the term "cloud computing" is totally meaningless and useless? No, on the contrary: by grouping this collection of trends, best practices and architectural patterns under the one term, it has gained enormous momentum. Cloud computing has become the name of a type of IT that integrates the latest thinking. It triggers the IT industry, and with it IT users worldwide, to rethink some of their practices and move towards a more rational and robust kind of IT. Instead of saying "you need to think about virtualization" *and* "you need to think about cost models for IT that align better with business decisions" *and* "you need to think about agility and speed of provisioning," all of that is combined into one: you need to think about the cloud. Down the line, the elements most relevant for you will pop up, while the "perfect" cloud serves as an ideal to strive for. Will cloud computing be the end of the line? Most likely not. The next post-cloud view will probably include even more and greater viewpoints on business and IT, without taking away any of the truths about cloud computing, much like cloud computing succeeded SOA by incorporating it.

2.4 Everybody is Pushing You to the Cloud

The IT ecosystem as a whole plays a part in any technological innovation. To understand why cloud computing is now on every agenda, one has to examine what is driving the vendors and the service providers.

Software vendors love the cloud model. First, it creates new ways to sell their software. Second, it creates a recurring revenue stream. Third, they expect that it offers new ways to lock users into some proprietary platform, system or data format. At the same time, some vendors are scared of the change, because the new model may decrease their profit margins or give new competitors an entry into the market.

Service providers see cloud computing not only as a new opportunity for consulting, migrations, and integration projects, but also as a new way to get "close" to their clients. Offering a service instead of a product means a continuing relationship instead of a one-project deal. At the same time, traditional service providers may look at this development with some reserve, for the risk of cannibalizing existing revenue seems very real. In a world where everybody is using commoditized cloud services, how much custom development business remains?

Then there are the IT industry analysts, who see cloud concepts as delivering on the promises made during the SOA hype. Analysts are a bit more cautious this time around, stating that cloud computing remains a major trend but that mainstream adoption may be slower than initially anticipated.

Within the organization, some forces are also favoring the cloud. Technical IT people are finding "web services" throughout their working environments, making it seductively easy to include external IT components in corporate solutions. The business side of the organization may start to consider cloud services on their own, attracted by the simplicity and ease of provisioning. And of course the CIO and CFO have their own reasons for being interested in the cloud. They may be looking to improve their time to market, make use of new functionality from the cloud, or simply better align the costs and benefits of IT. For business users, cloud products and services have clear attractions: self-provisioning promises solutions without the need to involve the IT department!

2.5   Cloud is for the People

Thanks to Web 2.0 and the many consumer-oriented solutions that are freely available on the web, the face of IT itself is changing. Business users have little patience any more for lengthy implementations with complicated decision processes. As private users they have become used to opening their browser and simply signing up for enjoyable and useful services. It has become commonplace for individuals to register for free conference calling, meeting places, document sharing, email, video hosting, mapping services or even personalized dashboards or content-management platforms. Creating or configuring a recruiting website no longer involves IT. In some companies, CRM systems have been set up without ever involving the IT department.

The CIO and enterprise architects are very slowly warming to the idea, but the reality is that the expectations for corporate IT departments have already changed dramatically. Users expect similar service and speed of deployment from the IT department that they now get on the public Internet.

> **A sunny day ... with no clouds**
>
> In the personal sphere, it's hard to imagine what our digital life would look like without cloud services. Most likely our email would be gone. There would be no YouTube or any other video-sharing site. Pictures we uploaded to Flickr or Picasa would be gone. Our online backup solution would no longer work, and even many multiplayer games would stop working. How often would you use a computer if your Internet connection were down? If the sun were shining without a cloud in the sky, what would you do?

Ultimately, this is a good thing: it should improve the long-sought alignment between business and IT, and it will let business make better decisions as to where to spend money on IT. Using a market model, business users can see the service and associated cost and make a decision as to whether to buy (or rent) it or not. Simple as that! Even though the CIO may worry about integration, security, auditing, and so on, the IT provisioning experience itself is seductively simple.

The first examples of user-initiated cloud solutions were point solutions that needed little or no integration. With the growth of the market, more solutions are becoming available that are more industry specific, more integrated into the business processes and provide true business value. These cloud services are not just technology services; they are starting to include complete business processes packaged as services. Video hosting is a fairly technical, non-specific process, but a recruiting process or expense management, for example, are true business processes that can now be outsourced to the cloud.

2.6   Of All Those Affected, the CIO Feels It Most

The role of the CIO is one that is under a lot of debate: should he be an operational manager, the driver of innovation, or part of the board? How do CIO and CTO relate, or are they one and the same? In any situation, the CIO will be the one responsible for providing business with the right IT support, preferably at the lowest price. In the past, many CIO's were simply told to cut their budget year after year, while keeping the business running. This has left some companies in the "skeletal" situation of "stripped down" IT where little capacity is available for systemic changes, quality improvement or innovation at all.

With the emergence of cloud computing, both the operational side (running the business) and the innovation side (building the business) are changing:

- Self-provisioning users ask for support, guidance and training rather than top-down policies set out by the IT department. Reshaping the enterprise architecture approach to reflect this shift will require significant change.
- The focus in the IT department shifts from offering products and trying to keep control to offering services and facilitating their use by the organization. A more empowered management style would make sense.
- The demand from the business for nicely contained, reusable services will grow. This fuels the debate between modernizing existing applications versus adopting SOA as a leading architectural style. If a user can set up a new mobile website in a matter of minutes, why does it take the IT department months to make the old systems mobile-enabled?
- The competition from large vendors providing cheaper email, hosting or other solutions will bring new budgetary pressures (and the need to find compelling reasons for not moving these elements into the cloud).
- Pay-per-use invites new costing models for IT.
- The cloud introduces yet another option to be considered in any buy-versus-build decision, with many new complexities that may make comparisons difficult. Careful planning, including identifying assumptions and scenarios, becomes essential.
- The cloud brings new power to IT, although few people yet appreciate its full potential. The CIO should take this opportunity to explore how this new innovative capacity can position the company ahead of the competition.

The emergence of the cloud could mean that the CIO will treat the internal IT department as "just another provider" and try to measure them against the same criteria as external providers: quality, efficiency, reliability, cost, speed of provisioning, *etc.* As soon as an external provider is better than the internal, should the external provider take over? Or maybe it's not that simple. Did we actually learn some lessons from the heyday of outsourcing?

Figure 2.1 (Widder 2010)

2.7 "Short-Term Cloud Thinking" Will Cost You More Than It Returns

Both the era of outsourcing and the era of the PC have taught us valuable lessons about the risks that come with some of these changes: once control is handed over to someone else, it may be hard to get it back; and once something becomes fragmented, it quickly becomes costly and also hard to consolidate. A plaque on the wall of any manager should read: "Don't make long-term commitments just for short-term reasons."

As a side-note on the subject of consolidation, virtual machines have been touted as a great way to counter the effect of the PC explosion. As a result of the sudden availability of cheap hardware and software, small servers or even desktops throughout the organization were running their own little tasks. Once they were turned into "virtual machines," they could all be brought back to the datacenter and run on virtual hardware while performing the same task: it saves money on hardware and it gives the illusion of integration. Of course, this is only an illusion: the silos, bad architecture, redundancies, *etc.* of the situation remain intact. Although virtual machines may require less hardware initially, they are so easy to create that the total number of "machines" will likely exceed the previous capacity.

The same thing is happening with the cloud: it's easy, readily available and often inexpensive. It's hard to prevent the impending rapid expansion and fragmentation, even though we see it long before it happens. Most IT organizations don't even have a cloud or SaaS strategy. For example, in an *InformationWeek Analytics* survey of 131 SaaS customers, 59 percent say it's a point solution, not a long-term strategy (Soat 2010).

Pick the low-hanging fruit? Yes! Forget about structure, long-term agility, integration? No! The adoption and governance of anything cloud-related must be guided by the enterprise architecture team. If not, in a couple of years the corporate data could be spread across many places, the company might be relying on way too many unreliable partners, the whole conglomerate of internal and external IT may have become impossible to change, and the benefits that the cloud once promised will have turned into liabilities. If you are serious about cloud computing, it should be a long-term vision and strategy. Going to the cloud is not a short-term visit, but a long-term structured journey.

2.8 There Is One Internet, But There Are Many Clouds

The people-oriented Internet of hyperlinked webpages feels highly integrated: with one web browser anyone can visit millions of pages, videos, pictures and the like. Most of the Internet conforms to the same architecture. Naturally, one hopes that the same simplicity applies with cloud services provided over the Internet or using Internet technology. Ideally, services should "link" to each other to compose business processes that suit the user. Services like recruitment, filling all sorts of HR forms, even providing someone with email and a laptop could all be separate but linked to comprise the whole on-boarding process.

The reality is that there is not one cloud: the lack of standards makes integration more difficult than creating a hyperlink on a webpage. Most likely, any connection between different services needs to be forged manually. For example, synchronizing user login details across multiple platforms is not easy. If multiple services run on the same cloud platform (for example, the Amazon cloud platform or Force.com), it will be a bit easier, but still not a trivial task. And connecting (let alone switching) from one platform to another is definitely not a seamless process yet. Basic technology for connecting and sending data may be there (HTTP and XML), but transactions, semantics, authentication, timing, *etc.* all need to be manually created.

As a consequence, "the cloud" should be read as shorthand for "a collection of disparate cloud services." Over time, we can expect either the service providers themselves or additional "integration in the cloud" providers to fill the gaps. New and traditional middleware companies are trying to cater to this need, but few standards exist even between them.

The conclusion at this time is that in the immature cloud market, selecting a cloud provider warrants some careful consideration. Unfortunately, this takes away a bit from the easy provisioning and speed of change.

2.9 First Stop: Hybrid Cloud

Organizations looking to use the cloud theme for a quick gain will first establish an internal, private cloud. Perhaps building on previous virtualization projects, it makes sense to apply the concepts to the organization's own datacenter first before including external resources.

The most likely scenario that companies foresee is that a part of IT will run internally and a part will run in the public cloud, with the option in between of a "virtual private cloud." In a virtual private cloud, the IT hardware physically resides at a hosting provider but it is dedicated to you. In this "single-tenant" situation, the hardware would not be shared with others. This is different from the public cloud, where resources are shared among the clients. The virtual private cloud offers some of the benefits of cloud without the risks associated with going public all the way, and is very similar to working with a traditional ASP or hosting provider.

Ideally, combining internal and external services forms a "hybrid" cloud: a well-integrated cloud where external resources would be available when internal resources reach their limits (often called "cloud bursting"). When the "on premise" servers are nearing their maximum performance capability, external servers jump in and take part of the load. When internal data storage reaches its capacity, external storage is available instantly. A "hybrid" situation is therefore more than simply combining internal and external. It adds a layer of management and integration on top.

Another mixed form is where certain tasks or workloads are in the cloud, while others remain on premise. In this situation, it's all about integration and maintaining features like transaction integrity and regular backups (and restores!) over the mix of internal and external services. Here too, "hybrid" is more than simply having a bunch of internal and external services that don't talk to each other.

It's still early days, but one can imagine a cloud governance layer that acts on a set of rules that combine business, IT and financial stakes to determine the behavior of the hybrid cloud.

But is this a desirable state of IT? Why not move all the way? What is keeping companies back? There are already some companies that have no internal IT at all: they have outsourced some parts in the traditional way, they use cloud services intensively and they work closely with other service providers in their ecosystem. Some companies don't even provide their own people with hardware anymore, leaving employees to choose their own laptop and mobile phone. What is holding you back?

2.10 **Sorry, You Don't Have a Private Cloud Just Yet**

Not many companies have even a full-fledged internal cloud just yet: they may have virtualized the hardware, but this is just the first step. The reality will be that for an increasing number of IT functions, the internal IT will compete with external providers.

The external providers are using their economies of scale to drive down all operational costs: self-provisioning is very nice for the speed of deployment, but the initial driver was simply to decrease human intervention. The numbers can be astounding: the number of people operating a server is getting close to zero. Google has been said to only have one administrator for 20,000 servers and is aiming for one person per 100,000 servers (Bias 2010). That is the kind of efficiency that internal IT will be competing against, and to achieve it you need automation. For a cost-effective private cloud you need to optimize and automate as many IT processes as you can, thereby automatically increasing agility and transparency. There would be very little variable cost: the cost is comprised of the hardware, licenses and network, with virtually no cost in human resources.

Ultimately you may introduce the final element of your private cloud: a per-use costing model where business users pay for IT resources based on actual usage. With these three elements in place, the private cloud would be complete: virtualization, full automation (*i.e.* self service) and pay-per-use.

Every step along the way has value, and taking one step at a time makes it achievable. Virtualization saves on hardware, automation saves on people cost and pay-per-use makes for better business-aligned IT investments, provided that business users are also learning how to invest strategically in IT.

2.11 **Alas, the Cloud May Not Be So Green After All**

There is an idea that cloud computing will make IT "green," which is related to the concept of improving economies of scale with regard to people per server: through economies of scale and better utilization, a more energy-efficient and eco-friendly IT will be possible.

The discussion around the value of greener technology is interesting in itself, since many companies seem primarily interested in the money they can save. (Have you ever seen a company publicly state that "we are spending a lot more on IT, but it has become a lot more environmentally friendly"?). Regardless of the motivation behind it, the ambition to save energy on IT is a valid one: continuing current trends would lead to a situation where energy and cooling will make up the main cost of IT.

But will the cloud make IT green? Or will something else happen? History teaches us that with the commoditization of technology, efficiency rises, but at the same time, cost falls and it becomes easier to use it. Old-fashioned economics still holds true: lower prices will increase the demand. So while the amount of energy spent "per task" may decline dramatically thanks to cloud services, one can expect the number of tasks being sent into the cloud to increase. Compare this to the search engines on the Internet: datacenters grew more efficient, increasing the number of servers and leading to more and better services. The end result is that Google most likely uses more power year after year (not information they like to share) (Leake 2009).

The only truly green IT coming from the cloud are the datacenters that use energy from solar, wind and other renewable sources. Thus, in a roundabout way, the discussion around green IT and the cloud will bring attention to the topic, which in turn may lead to more service providers choosing to offer truly green IT.

2.12 Your Clients, Employees and Competitors Are Ahead of You Already!

Individual users have grown accustomed to cloud computing in the consumer space and have accepted the risks and usability quirks of online services. Your employees, your clients and most likely your competitors are using cloud services every day.

If you are not yet picking the low-hanging fruit, your company is already lagging behind. If you have not yet explored cloud options in a pilot or small project, your competition is ahead of you. If, for example, the software development team is not using the cloud for their Linux projects, they are wasting corporate resources.

These low-hanging fruits of cloud computing are waiting to be picked:

- Software development and test environments.
- Short-term, high performance needs for large one-off calculations or for big conversion tasks. Sudden peak loads on public facing servers can be offloaded into the cloud.
- Temporary solutions. Any environment that is temporary with little or no need to be integrated and contains no sensitive data, which may be a campaign-related web service, a bridging solution to facilitate a company merger or a plan in the event of a natural disaster.
- Any services that, inherent in their functionality, are best in the cloud and outside of the organization, which may be public video hosting, conference calling, file sharing, channel collaboration or recruitment.

For start-up companies, but also for companies in developing countries, the cloud model presents the ideal way to use technology, offering great functionality quickly with extremely low upfront investment. Competition from them can be sudden and strong. With no burden of legacy systems, they are poised to take advantage of what's available online. They could cobble together an online CRM, a content management tool, email, an inventory management service and an invoicing service, then presto! They are in business!

And you may find yourself lagging, but on the other hand, if you were betting everything on the cloud already, you would be among the leaders. There is still time to catch the wave.

2.13 We Have More Technology Than We Can Muster Today

New opportunities that break the model are beyond our imagination. Companies are just beginning to explore what it means to use everything that is available from the cloud. How can we best use these new collaborative tools? What can we do with huge public datasets, or extensive datasets shared among channel partners? What does it mean when every individual user in the enterprise can command computing power that is equivalent to that of a supercomputer? New automations, new patterns and new organizations will arise that know how to benefit from this new reality. Two people in a garage may start a new company that rapidly overtakes a well-established incumbent player.

The reality is that we have so much technology at our fingertips that technology itself is no longer the inhibitor: it might be our own imagination or simply the end user's capacity for change. This is where the cloud needs to be an inspiration and not simply a solution: the cloud not only helps solve some of the great challenges of IT within organizations, it also makes new things possible.

2.14 Conclusion

Surely, many more things could be said about the cloud: about the new opportunities that it brings into reach and the effects that it might have going forward. It may not be the solution to all IT challenges that we would wish it to be, but it does advance our options and create new business opportunities. The cloud is not something you can ignore. It needs to be examined, weighed and tested. These 12 bold statements show the potential and the hope, but also the disclaimers of reality in a complex technological world. There will be a sustained need for smart people with vision, ideas and a way to make things happen. Only with them will the cloud and technology in general be of any use to an organization.

In the next chapter, we'll examine this relation between business and technology more closely, and we'll dive into what is called *business technology*, for which cloud computing is a great enabler.

For New Generation of IT Leaders, There is No Option to Cloud Computing
Bambuser Founder Among Those For Whom the Cloud is a No-Brainer

Throughout the business world, IT execs are grappling with whether to commit to cloud computing or not. They ooh and ah over its numerous business benefits, fret over its perceived weaknesses, and test the waters by using niche cloud services or entrusting low-priority applications to cloud service providers.

And as they do, tech-savvy 20-somethings collectively wonder, "huh?"

Måns Adler is one such 20-something. The founder of Swedish mobile video service Bambuser represents a new wave of technologists who come at IT from a fresh perspective. They eschew the philosophies and terminologies of traditional IT—"cloud computing" among them—and instead simply opt to use the technologies that are abundantly available to them so they can focus on building consumer services rather than IT environments.

The most obvious such resource is the world of cloud-based services. Just don't call it the cloud, or Adler might not follow you. He considers "cloud computing" to be a stale IT term that means little to him. "From my younger perspective, there's never been a different way of going about it," he says. "It was so clear from the beginning."

Cloud Based Services Abound From the Start

The beginning was 2007, when Adler started up Bambuser and began work on the company's service, which enables video to be broadcast over the web in near real time from a mobile phone. The idea that he might have to invest money in servers and software to create an environment for building and delivering Bambuser's service never even occurred to Adler; rather, he and his founding team just went online and found just about all the tools they needed.

You name it, and Bambuser uses a free cloud service for it. Email? Bambuser relies exclusively on Gmail. Phone service? No reason not to use Skype. Word processing and document sharing? Google Apps works great. Create a private social network for real-time communication and collaboration? Yammer filled in nicely. Usage tracking? Thank you, Google Analytics.

In fact, Bambuser pays for very few of the technologies it uses. It pays a nominal monthly fee for FogBugz, an online bug-reporting service; it pays about $1,500 a month to a Swedish ISP for access to a single server that hosts Bambuser's development environment, and it spends between $2,000 and $6,000 per month to have its peak video traffic routed through Amazon Web Services' Elastic Compute Cloud.

That means it costs just a few thousand dollars a month to run Bambuser's whole operation, an eye-popping number that illustrates the value the cloud brings to startups that can make the best use of the platform. And best of all, Bambuser users not only wouldn't care, they wouldn't have the slightest idea they're using a cloud-based service themselves. "As long as you get it right and the users get a great experience," says Adler, "they'll never even think about whether it's a cloud service or not."

Bambuser's Cloud-Friendly 20-Somethings: IT Staff of the Future

Given the company's reliance on cloud services, it should come as no surprise that Adler likes to fill jobs with IT workers in their mid-20s who are like-minded to him, ones who are accustomed to using Web-based administrative tools. In fact, all but one of the company's dozen employees is in their 20s. The lone exception is CEO Hans Eriksson, a 40-something brought in partly to balance out the staff's youth. Yet even Eriksson isn't interested in whether a technology Bambuser uses is a cloud service or not. "For him, the only thing that matters is that it works," says Adler.

The idea of a technology staff that doesn't think about whether to use the cloud or not, but instead just charges ahead with Web-based applications and services, is a new concept. It challenges the typical IT approach of carefully evaluating options, running risk-benefit analyses, seeking approval from the board, and undergoing extensive test periods.

It also signals that once today's 20-something are making the big IT decisions, cloud computing no longer will be one of several options—it will be the ONLY option.

3 Business Innovation Through Cloud Computing

3.1 Introduction

Part of the promise of cloud computing is that technology will become more business-driven. In this chapter we will discuss the interaction between business and technology, and we will show that a shift is taking place from information technology to business technology, a shift from IT as a separate entity to something embedded into everything we do. Cloud computing is part of this shift. The chapter will describe the effects, and how you can prepare for this change to create the real business agility that cloud is promising.

3.2 From Information Technology to Business Technology

Technology* is part of everyday life, in business as much as in our personal life. Take away the applications, email, networks and Internet from any organization and it would come to a standstill almost immediately. This is more so now than ever before: in the days of phone and fax, we could probably do fine without technology for a day or two. The difference today is more than just greater dependency: we are no longer doing the same things. Supported with technology we are starting to do new things that we simply could not do without that technology. And now that technology has found its way into all parts of our organization, we are asking new things of it. Looking closer at what we now demand of information technology, it becomes clear that cloud computing is a good model for provisioning and paying for technology. It will give a boost to whatever we are doing.

---

*   This chapter does not delve into the hard "machine" technologies that may be part of manufacturing or operations in some companies. While there is a trend of convergence, the dynamics for that kind of technology are different from what is described here.

Designing a new car

When thinking about technology and business, one could think of them as two parts that together make up an organization. Compare this to the early automobile industry, where the construction of a car was done in two parts: the first part was a frame, a sturdy framework with wheels, power train and suspension; attached to that was the second part, the coachwork of the car. The coachwork actually contained most of the visible car, but did not bear any load: the body did not contribute to the strength or basic structure of the car. This is no longer true. Modern cars are different: the body of the car is part of the structure itself. Take away the body and there is not enough structure left to hold the rest in place. The unibody, or monocoque, construction method is now the primary construction method for passenger cars, making much lighter and cheaper cars a reality.

Cyborg organizations

Similarly, modern organizations are not businesses on top of (or supported by) technology, nor are they a frame of technology-free conceptual business processes to which technology is applied. Instead they have become interwoven, integrated. Take away the technology and there is nothing left. Real-time inventory and restocking of a supermarket chain can only exist with technology. Collaboration across great distances can only be performed if the right communication technology is in place. Any bank that offers mobile banking, Internet banking or automated transactions is now selling services that are in fact technology services. You could say that organizations have become *cyborg* organizations: by adopting more and more technology, organizations have become technological in their very essence and fabric. Technology is part of an organization's basic operation (for example, how we communicate internally or how we pay) but also part of the competitive advantage (how we approach our customers and how we define new products). For some companies, it goes even further, and technology has become an integral part of what they sell.

Technology defines how we do and are able to do almost everything, from marketing to manufacturing, from billing to human resource management. For people who have only joined the workforce in the past 5 years, it's impossible to imagine what a company was like before there was such widespread technology (or with email only). Consider all the ways we use technology:

- Defining new products, through simulation and research, crowdsourcing innovation, and measuring satisfaction and ratings.
- Manufacturing, using not just machines but production automation, configurable machines and detailed statistics for process optimization.
- Delivering services, using web-based interaction for customization and customer intimacy, knowledge management, collaboration and delivery.
- Automating the supply chain, using real-time insight to manage and synchronize inventory, billing, *etc.*
- Marketing, using online campaigns, social media, video hosting or websites. When interacting with your clients, how much is technology and how much is face time with real people?
- Communicating inside the company, using intranet, wiki's or internal blogs, digital newsletters, *etc.*
- Managing human resources with self-service tools for core HR processes.
- Billing, using direct links to your bank, payment providers and other service providers.
- Working with partners, with collaboration tools, interconnected systems and shared data.
- Creating strategy and making decisions based on trends, business intelligence and advanced analytics.

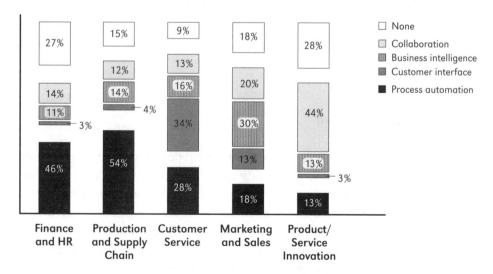

Figure 3.1: A breakdown of how and how much different types of processes in an organization can be enabled with technology (The Corporate Executive Board Company 2010)

Technology may be especially visible in larger enterprises that focus on services, but it is also making a difference in smaller businesses. Even if you are a manufacturer dealing with lots of manual labor, the logistics, planning, modeling and sales involve technology today. And as with every innovation, if your company is not doing it, some competitor will try to beat you to it.

Technology is even part of products

A recent lesson is that the perceived value of physical goods is created through a technology layer that enhances the product. Producers are using the digital layer to increase brand awareness and change (improve) perception of the product through games, extra information, virtual reality, loyalty rewards programs, and so forth. Car makers earn money with options like navigation systems or crash-assistance services. So called quick response (QR) codes in brochures or product manuals connect the buyers' mobile device directly to online resources that provide information or social networking for the user, while giving the producer the added benefit of greater customer intimacy.

For producers this is one of the ways to counter the commoditization of physical products: innovate through branding and the digital experience, all part of the so-called "experience economy." It perhaps goes without saying that the advances in technology determine the possibilities and competition in this space. The iPhone launched many new opportunities. Cheap online video created a new channel. The availability of virtually endless (cloud) resources has yet to be completely utilized.

Email as a special case

The examples above don't even mention the most pervasive technology: email. It is both trivial ("of course everybody relies on email") and very relevant. Thanks to cloud computing, several alternatives to email are springing up that challenge the necessity of email. One of the oft described generational differences between the "working" population and the college population is that the latter has stopped using email altogether, replacing it with Facebook wall posts, Twitter, instant messaging, text messaging and various other means of communication. (And all of these tools are cloud!) So while email may be everywhere, thanks to the cloud, alternatives may present themselves that will change the way you do internal communication, distribute a message or gather feedback on a document. Mobile computing is set to be the next big game changer that will be cross functional, touching upon everything we do: do you check your BlackBerry on vacation? That is just the beginning.

New business patterns

When you try to imagine how technology could change your business, it's sometimes hard to look beyond the current state. But the real opportunities may lie just *outside the box*: What is your business model, and why? What happens if some technology becomes extremely cheap and easy to provision? What happens if it costs next to nothing to resell the products or services from others? What happens in a business world where there are no more secrets, and links are free? Real innovation often occurs through the adoption of completely new business models. An interesting way to think about this is to explore modern business patterns. For example, could you use technology to embrace a long-tail model (Anderson 2006) for some of your activities? Could you start selling niche products that generate as much revenue as your current top 3 products? Could you mass-customize?

Embracing business technology for even greater goals

We are not yet fully realizing the opportunities that exist today. It's easy to be blinded by the small everyday issues so that the larger goal stays out of reach. Now that businesses and public organizations are "wired" and the cloud has emerged as a collection of Internet platforms and tools for connecting, integration and sharing of data and processes, it has become possible to think about the bigger issues that are going unaddressed. IBM, for one, has launched a campaign named "Smarter Planet" where pervasive technologies and eco-systems of companies are urged to work together in solving societal problems in the fields of transportation, healthcare, environment, education, *etc*. The main thought is, what could we accomplish if we all aim to solve a bigger issue together, crossing organizational boundaries and creating these systems of systems?

3.3 Are You Already a Business Technology Company?

It is one thing to have technology embedded into everything we do as an organization. It is quite another to have true business technology (BT): a view of technology that fits the reality where technology is no longer seen as quasi-independent of the rest of the organization. So, are you there yet? There is no single test that will tell you if you are using true BT, but there are some indicators that will give you an idea.

	IT	BT
Primarily responsible for IT selection and provisioning is ...	IT department	Business, with the IT department as broker
Technology is implemented through ...	Projects	Self service or iterative provisioning
Main focus of the IT dept is to ...	Build things right	Build only the right things
CIO's role is ...	Responsible for creation and operation of technology while reducing cost	Managing a portfolio of services, some internal and some external
Technology is marketed by talking about ...	Features & functionality	Business outcomes
Enterprise architects are ...	Famous for saying "No" and causing delay to business projects	Famous for saying "Yes," facilitating, accelerating and coming up with business ideas
Functions related to technology are found ...	Only in IT	Mostly in IT department for technical roles, but with business analysts, workflow and process management functions in the business
Innovation is ...	New technology	Joint business innovation
Expected value from technology is to ...	Increase productivity	Increase market share & revenue
Business strategy is ...	Focused on physical products and services first	Focused on the digital dimension of products and services first
Business executives' knowledge of technology is ...	Basic, as a user	Extensive, with deep insight into trends and business opportunities
Marketing, business and technology operate ...	Each in their own domain	Closely integrated
Technology is measured by looking at ...	Usage, load, uptime	Customer interactions, transactions, revenue

Table 3.1: IT versus BT

3.4 How Business Technology and Cloud Computing Are a Perfect Match

This new view of technology as part of the business makes high demands on how we deal with technology in the enterprise. Cloud computing is a model that fits surprisingly well with the expectations set by the BT approach:

- *Business Metrics*. Business is all about sales, revenue, reducing cost and increasing profit. Success is defined by the long-term profitable growth that is realized and measured in return on investment. These are the measurements that are important, so they should be the basis of the IT metrics. The metrics should not be some vague, hard to estimate calculation of possible cost and ROI, but straightforward calculations, like "60 cents of every transaction goes to cover IT costs" or, "for every x% increase in sales, we will have y% increase in IT cost." This is exactly the realm of cloud computing: pay for what you use, and scale as needed. Regardless of whether the technology is coming from a private or a public cloud, this is the model that resonates within the business.

- *Business Terminology*. We need to stop talking about technology in technical terms but think in terms of business outcomes. This was already an issue when we were still talking about IT and *alignment* within the organization, but the advent of business technology has focused the issue. While the business side is becoming more tech-savvy, IT is becoming more business savvy, changing the uneven balance of the conversation and making it easier to bridge the gap between them. In the end, IT will need to shift more towards the business side than vice versa. Likewise, when designing IT, segmentations that are made for technical reasons do not fit well with the expectations of end users. Business processes and business functions are the relevant entities to address, leading the conversation primarily to business services from the cloud rather than to the more infrastructural or technical cloud components.

- *Meaningful Business Innovation versus Common Infrastructure*. If you use expensive, custom-built technology that does no more than support your basic non-differentiating functions, chances are that the competition will get the better of you. They are investing in the next great product or service, the next level of client intimacy or the next great way to do interactive marketing. This was already the promise of SOA (loosen things up so that commodity parts can be replaced by package solutions or services). With cloud services, the promise has come closer to being a reality: money spent on technology is expected to create new business opportunities. Swapping out custom systems for readymade cloud services should free up budget and time for true business innovation. The business case for NOT commoditizing a large part of your IT every year should be very strong and constantly challenged to warrant the extra operational cost.

- *Business Ownership and Self Provisioning.* The core premise of business technology is that business takes ownership of technology. For this to happen, business has to be supported and educated on the possibilities of technology, which is the role of the IT department. Business must also be engaged in the provisioning model. The business technology ideal would be for technology to be self provisioned, with no IT department involvement. In reality, IT does have a valuable role, and will act more like the accounting department, as integral to the business function and not a "service department" only. For sake of future stability, integration, security and so forth, the IT department will need to stay involved in a broker/support role. This is exactly how cloud makes a difference: making it easier and more transparent to provision new technology. Many cloud services are well described on an open market where any user can evaluate their relative function and cost instantly.

- *Extreme Flexibility.* In a commercial business, reducing time-to-market and capitalizing quickly on opportunities is essential. In government, a quick show of success is important in a political cycle. When you're working for a non-profit organization, quick response to what's in the news makes a difference in visibility, fundraising and the execution of your mission. It's the holy grail of IT: be more adaptive to change. More precisely, the challenge is to *stay* adaptive to change over time, even after weathering many previous changes. A quagmire of prior quick fixes usually prevents any future quick changes. Big up-front investments or "sunk costs" tend to paralyze and prevent you from moving away from prior choices. High switching costs lock you up. Yet if we want technology and business to operate as one, something needs to give. Cloud helps by making it easier to move in and out of technology solutions, but there remains a major challenge for any CIO who must enforce some structure and map some architecture onto it so that the agility of today doesn't become the limitation of tomorrow.

The "old" IT as a corporate conscience

Business doesn't care about architecture. They should, but they don't. Short-term gain almost always wins over long-term considerations, especially if the short-term opportunity is revenue and the long-term consideration is (perceived as) a technology issue. A quick and dirty solution doesn't sound so bad if we can earn some extra money, right?

Traditionally the CIO, responsible for enterprise (*IT*) architecture, was the only one who worried about reducing complexity and trying to limit the number of variations in order to remain agile and responsive. Now business is assuming a more proactive role with regard to technology provisioning, so part of this responsibility falls to them, too. You can self-provision whatever you want, but you will have to bear the consequences if it doesn't integrate well or proves to be very resistant to change.

The role of an enterprise architecture practice should be exactly that: not just guiding technology but guiding the organization as a whole. To ensure security, integration and even cost control in a more distributed, fragmented world, the importance of enterprise architecture will increase. This should be founded on a principle-based architecture guiding the decision-making process, and not a traditional blue-prints based plan that everybody needs to follow. The architecture principles should be light and easy to digest, yet robust enough to help to keep complexity down (and agility up). This is one of the areas where the CIO needs to play a proactive role. Initiating the discussions within the organization that focus these issues in business terms: what process or function has become a commodity, and what's your business case to NOT commoditize the technology part of it? Or, if you had to give up one piece of technology in your organization, what would it be?

What this all means to the IT department

Most IT departments today are not ready for the agility and business involvement that is required in a true business technology company. To grow in this direction, cloud will inject some agility in the technology provisioning and cost models, but other aspects will need to be addressed separately:

* Educate business executives on the basics of IT that are needed to become technologically knowledgeable business people. In the "old" days, anyone in the business needed to know at least the basics of finance, marketing and HR. Today, we add technology to that list. Check any current MBA curriculum if you are still in doubt of what skills the future business leaders will be bringing. On the IT side, this means it is necessary to adopt a way of talking about technology that is more understandable to business.

- Align the speed of change in IT to the speed of change on the business side. Processes and people in IT need to match whatever else is going on. Employ process optimization within IT, applying Lean, CMM (Capability Maturity Model) or ITIL (IT Infrastructure Management Library), which are important levers to be able to speed up the business instead of slowing it down.
- Before creating a cloud strategy, you will need to understand your business strategy first, and then determine the role technology must play in your organization. The cloud strategy will then be much less about platforms or technical decisions and much more linked to the innovation of business processes and, for example, your business process outsourcing (BPO) strategy.

It is important to note that although the scope and relevance of technology has increased, this does not automatically imply a larger role for the traditional IT department. Delegation, shared responsibility with the business and automation will more likely shrink the IT department. On the other hand, rogue IT—IT that is outside the control of the IT department—is still not desirable. When an organization continues to have a lot of rogue IT, it could be a symptom of an IT department that is perceived as unresponsive, incapable or inflexible. Not exactly the intimacy and collaboration you would expect in a business technology company. In fact, Forrester Research mentions a good organizational collaborative culture as one of the success factors for business technology (Cameron 2009).

3.5 Conclusion

We truly live in a digital age, with *digital natives* and digital products and services. It's no wonder that technology is embedded in everything organizations do. As we realize how prevalent technology is, we see that every technological innovation can create many new paths for organizations to grow and improve. Cloud computing is one of these innovations, and one that will have far-reaching effects on how organizations operate and how they are structured. If you want to be in business, you have to understand finance, management and strategy. We all know that. But if you want to stay in business you have to really understand technology. The future of organizations will be determined by the presence of tech-savvy business executives who bridge the cognitive gap between IT and business, and who constantly drive technology-enabled, meaningful business innovation.

To make this more concrete, we can examine the financial model of IT and the changes that cloud computing is bringing. This we will do in the next chapter, where the economics of IT will be explained, and the different roles and payment types that are associated with them.

Cloud Computing Reshaping
Early Stage Venture Capital Investing
Smaller Investment Requirements
Yield "More Shots on Goal"

One of the unanticipated ways cloud computing is impacting the technology world is this: It's completely rewriting the rules of early-stage venture capital investing.

From driving down the costs of building a company to enabling massive scalability out of the gate, the cloud has resulted in venture firms seeing deals requiring smaller capital requirements, but more of them. That cloud computing is a big draw for venture investors should come as no surprise, as it enables young companies to greatly reduce the time it takes to get their products to market.

"I just have to get in my car and drive up on the freeway and I'm going 80 mph right away," says Scott Orn, a principal at Silicon Valley venture firm Lighthouse Capital. "It's amazing."

It's a win/win scenario: young cloud companies needing less money to fund their initial pushes can reduce the amount of control and ownership they have to give up, and venture fund managers looking to make the most of their investment dollars in a tough economy get to take "more shots on goal," as Orn puts it.

Cloud's Impact Trickling Down, Affecting Investment Decisions

Orn, whose investment portfolio includes young cloud-related companies trying to break into both the corporate computing and consumer applications markets, says the smaller early-stage investment needs are having a trickle-down effect.

"The reduction in infrastructure costs and risk can ripple through the ecosystem and open up early stage investing for a whole new class of investors," he says. Orn points out that so-called "super-angels," or private investors who make larger, later investments than traditional seed angels, are now able to fund deals that previously would have required venture capital backing.

Meanwhile, Orn says the mere presence of cloud computing is altering investment decisions, as venture investors are more interested in companies that are leveraging cloud computing rather than getting bogged down in establishing their own IT operations. So, if a venture capitalist was faced with two companies offering equally great services, but one was using Amazon's Elastic Compute Cloud or some other mature cloud offering to meet its peak computing needs while the other was building its own data center, Orn insists the decision would be simple.

"You'd run away from the second company," he says. "It's table stakes; it's like coming to the table without an ante. That's how much people trust Amazon."

VCs Want Companies That Leverage the Cloud Rather Than Power It

That growing trust in cloud computing is a huge development. By encouraging the young companies of today to take advantage of the cloud, the venture community is, in effect, acting as a cloud advocate and ensuring its growth.

Ironically, though, venture investors are much more skittish when it comes to startups looking to actually become cloud providers. Startups looking to establish themselves as fully integrated cloud solutions face stiff competition from the big, established IT vendors, Orn says. And even those companies that address a cloud niche still often face too many questions about their future. "I wish we had more cloud companies to invest in," he says. "But they're very early in their lifecycles right now, and they haven't quite matured to the level we're playing at."

Any cloud provider startup hoping to secure venture funding should be focused on doing one thing very well, Orn says. If such a company can demonstrate that it has a disruptive technology that has the potential to define a new market, venture investors become much more interested. For instance, one of Orn's portfolio companies, Delphix, specializes in the largely untapped area of database virtualization.

But with the cloud provider market increasingly crowded, such companies are few and far between. Conversely, entrepreneurs are creating myriad innovative new services that leverage the cloud's low-cost, ready-made IT infrastructure. It's an exciting new startup business model for a venture capital industry in search of lower risk and faster returns.

"Instead of funding infrastructure costs, [venture investors] are actually funding real apps and business services," says Orn.

4 Cloud Economics

4.1 Introduction

"Just follow the money." This was the advice of the secret source Deep Throat to reporter Bob Woodward in the movie *All the President's Men*. Following the money can be a way to reveal the complex relations and interactions between different parties, which in the case depicted in the movie lead to the uncovering of the Watergate scandal. In this particular chapter we will also follow the money and bring light to the relations and interactions around cloud. We will demonstrate that cloud computing will have a significant effect on the business model of all economic agents in the IT market. The pressure to change is caused mainly by the shift from assets to services and the change from a license model to a subscription model. The resulting emergence of a more transparent marketplace for IT services is also a factor.

As we will discuss in this chapter the effect of cloud will be felt throughout the industry, by all parties: hardware providers, software providers, service providers as well as internal IT departments. Cloud computing has increased the number of ways these agents can collaborate, interact and charge for IT.

In this chapter, we will start to discuss the major shifts cloud computing is bringing. Then we will cover the effect these shifts have on the flow of money and goods between economic agents in the IT-market. Finally we will describe what is changing for each of these economic agents.

4.2 The Overall Impact of Cloud Computing

Cloud computing has a significant impact on the way hardware, software and services are produced, distributed and consumed. These changes will be discussed below.

From assets to services

Traditionally hardware and software have been produced, distributed and consumed as assets. Making use of such assets required an (often large) upfront capital investment by the consumer. In the cloud era, services become available that could be consumed on a pay-as-you-go basis. Capital investments in assets are absorbed by the provider and billed to the consumer on the basis of real usage. From the consumer's perspective, capital expenditure to acquire or develop assets is replaced by operating expenses associated with the use of services. The flip side of the coin is of course that the required capital expenditure shifts from the consumer to the provider.

From buying or leasing hardware to infrastructure as a service

Traditionally hardware has been bought or leased by organizations. Purchasing equipment is an investment that has a negative impact on the cash flow. Hardware is carried on the balance sheet as a long-term capital asset. Maintenance and depreciation costs are part of the income statement.

In the case of leased hardware, the investment is not taken upfront but as an operating expense. However, because a certain period for leasing has to be contractually agreed upfront, the implications remain the same as in the purchase scenario.

In the cloud era, hardware is no longer bought or leased but instead used as a service to which one can subscribe. The price paid depends on the number of times the service is actually provided. Because no upfront investment is necessary to make use of the service, hardware is no longer carried on the balance sheet and no depreciation is required (Schadler 2008). All costs become part of the income statement. Payments are simply made when the service is provided.

From a license model to a subscription model for software

Software is treated exactly the same as hardware in the cloud era. Software is also something one can subscribe to and use as a service. The difference with hardware is the way software is acquired traditionally. Software can either be custom-built or bought based on licenses. A license grants a right to one party to use material owned by the other party, and the material in this case is software. Often the license is limited to a number of users and/or a time period. One needs to pay a fee for the license, which is a capital expenditure. When software is custom-built one normally needs to pay for the total development investment upfront, which would also be a capital expenditure.

While the license model is already quite attractive for providers, the subscription model is even more so. With the subscription model, the costs a user would incur for switching to an alternative service can quickly become prohibitive, creating an effective lock-in. In that way, the service provider not only gets a recurring fee but one that is likely to continue for a long time.

The rise of a big transparent marketplace

As a consequence of the shift from assets to services, a more transparent and liquid marketplace is emerging. It is transparent in the sense that consumers are able to compare services and prices of different vendors. It is a liquid marketplace because the total trading capacity (of all services) is more scalable and thus provides ways to utilize that capacity better. Sharing capacity drives up efficiency of asset usage among cloud providers in the system and so drives down cost for all. A more transparent and liquid marketplace at the end will mean benefits for the users of this marketplace (the cloud consumers) in terms of finding the right service at a competitive price.

Usage-based pricing will drive the need to explicitly value IT services

Gartner's model for IT cost allocation (shown in Figure 4.1) suggests an evolution of IT chargeback from simple cost-allocation schemes to negotiated pricing to market-based pricing. Another level of evolution will see chargeback, which once only operated at the lower layers of IT (like storage, servers and bandwidth), moving into higher layers and using composite metrics that include all layers of the service, including the application (for example the "pay per click" on SAP transactions).

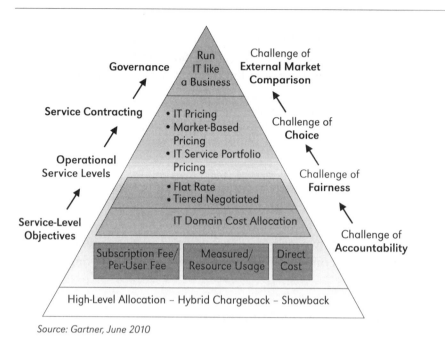

Source: Gartner, June 2010

Figure 4.1: Hierarchy for cost-allocation evolution

To some extent, the evolution towards the top of the pyramid will be driven by the desire of business to benchmark their internal IT relative to external service providers. Already today business executives can easily determine the cost of a transaction, the cost of an application service, or the cost of a gigabyte of storage through public cloud services. This market comparison will force IT to justify any price differences between the services they provide and comparable services that are publicly available. IT departments need to work hard to explain why the overall price for, say, a Windows server is 50% less per hour on Amazon Web Services than what internal IT costs. Internal "private" clouds will be particularly scrutinized by this continuous benchmarking against similar offerings from the public space. This will force private cloud providers to justify and quantify their added value in terms of security, compliance, service levels and support in comparison to the public marketplace.

The difference between build and run diminishes

Traditionally about 80% of the IT budget is consumed by running costs: costs to operate and maintain the current systems. This is the domain of IT, where business has little influence. IT normally charges these costs to the business on a lump sum basis, which is one of the reasons why the business perceives these costs as overhead.

The remaining 20% is spent on projects where new applications are built or package solutions are customized. Normally the business controls the build-costs and handles these as investments.

In the cloud era this will change. Software is used as a service, and once implemented, these services and the associated costs can be directly linked to the business users who asked for them. Depending on the number of business users or the number of transactions, for example, these business users can be charged directly for the use of the software. The costs for migration and implementation can be included in the usage price of a service. In this case all costs can be controlled by the business and the distinction between building and running costs becomes obscured.

4.3   The Impact of Cloud on the Flow of Goods and Money

The traditional flows

The traditional flow of IT services and money is shown in Figure 4.2. The business user requests services that are delivered by a provider (in most cases, the internal IT department) and pays a lump sum cost for these services.

Internal IT contracts different providers and pays them for the software, hardware and services. These providers are paid based on time, material or licenses.

How cloud impacts the flows

Figure 4.3 shows all the different ways cloud can impact the flow of services and money. The dark boxes and arrows indicate the changes.

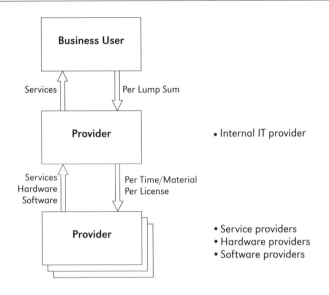

Figure 4.2: Traditional flow of services and money

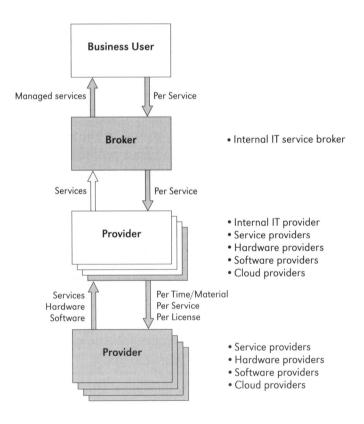

Figure 4.3: Flow of services and money in the cloud era

The main changes depicted in Figure 4.3 are:

- A cloud type of provider emerges. This is a new type of service provider that offers cloud-based services (which could be anything provided as a service) and is paid for the actual use of these services.
- A broker role emerges. Cloud computing offers more and different opportunities to acquire services. The number of providers will increase as will the different characteristics of these services (for example, the application programming interfaces). These different kind of services have to be offered to business users in a coherent and integrated way. That is where a broker function is required. This role is sometimes also referred to as the demand function of IT. Chapter 5 will elaborate on this subject.
- Business users will get managed services instead of a whole bunch of loose services. A managed service is a service that is delivered from a service catalogue and integrates different lower-level services into something that adds value for the business user.
- Business users are charged by the broker per service instead of in a lump sum. Business users will see a more direct relationship between what they consume and what they pay.
- The broker is charged per service instead of per time, per material or per license.
- Internal IT as a provider is no longer the single point of contact for its business users. That role is taken over by the broker function. Internal IT, on the supply side, has become a supplier that has to compete with external providers. Internal IT has to deliver services and charge for the consumption of these services. One of the options for internal IT is to transform into a private cloud provider, delivering cloud services that are so critical for the organization that they cannot be outsourced.
- A whole ecosystem of providers will emerge within an organizational context. For example, a SaaS provider is buying software and hardware from different providers to be able to offer a SaaS solution via a broker to business users. Different ways of acquiring goods and services will exist next to one another, resulting in different ways these goods and services will be charged.

Overall, the cloud will increase the number of options for how to deploy and charge for IT. In order to hide this increasing complexity for business users, the broker function will become more and more important. Chapter 5 will discuss the new IT constitution in more depth.

4.4 The Impact of Cloud on Different Types of Providers and Consumers

In the whole stack of producers and consumers of IT services, the following parties can be identified:
- Business users who consume services.
- Internal IT department, which produces and consumes services.
- Incumbent service providers who sell consultancy, technology and/or outsourcing services.
- Software providers who create software which is sold based on licenses.
- Hardware providers who sell computer equipment.
- Cloud providers who sell cloud services.

How does cloud computing affect the way these different parties produce and consume hardware, software and services?

Business users are in the driver's seat

With the increasing competition between service providers offering different kinds of services under different conditions and prices, the business users have the golden opportunity to reap potential benefits like more agility, more flexibility, cost savings and an improved time-to-market.

David Linthicum, a well-known cloud computing and SOA expert, wrote a blog about the real value of cloud computing, which is right on the money. He identifies three core values: self improvement, agility and time to operations.
"Now that cloud computing is in the mega-hype stage there are continuous attempts to define the true value of cloud computing for enterprises and government. Most of the time we talk about capital expenses versus operating expenses, and sometimes the concept of agility, including the elastic nature of cloud computing. So how should you evaluate the value of cloud computing in the context of your enterprise? The truth of the matter is, there are no hard and fast formulas we can leverage to compute the exact dollar benefit of any new type of technology application, including cloud computing. However, there are many aspects of this new model to consider to help determine the real value of cloud computing:
Self improvement is the value of taking a new look at your existing IT solutions. One of the things that cloud computing forces you to do is to examine your existing IT architecture and determine what works and what does not. Then, create a plan to

improve upon it as you relocate aspects of the existing architecture to the cloud. The value here is an improvement on the existing way things are done as you move from platform to platform. This value will be apparent no matter if you move to a cloud platform or not. We'll see many who brag about how the new cloud computing deployment is such a success and a cost saver, when the core value is really around the improvement in the architecture and not the movement into the cloud. However, I'll still count this as a true value of moving to the cloud.

Agility is the ability to change your IT solutions to better react to the needs of the business. The value of agility is nothing new; the degree of value will vary greatly from enterprise to enterprise. Cloud computing provides you with the ability to adjust solutions as the business or mission changes, allowing IT to scale up or down, and to do so in almost direct proportion to costs. Moreover, you can more quickly adjust by leveraging the cloud considering that purchasing hardware and software, as well as integration, has been factored out of the equation.

Time to operations is the ability to quickly get something up and running to meet the needs of the business. Related to agility, but not exactly the same, time to operations is the ability for IT to determine on Monday that we need additional storage to support a particular application, and they will have that storage system up and running in the cloud on Tuesday. Or, the ability to leverage Google App Engine to build an application to meet a business need, without having to wait for the hardware and software to be delivered and installed.

Finally, it's the ability to leverage a SaaS player, such as Salesforce.com or others, rather than go through the pain and expense of implementing an on-premise enterprise software package, most of which are famous for taking more time and money than originally expected. Notice that I've yet to mention capital expenses or operational expenses, which are innate to the values described above. I assume that you focus on self improvement, agility, and time to operations as the core value of cloud computing. You'll find that these factors serve you better in making a business case for cloud computing. They are the true values of the cloud." (Linthicum 2010)

If done correctly, cloud computing will certainly generate benefits for the business users. This requires a well-balanced approach between the business user who will drive the change and the internal IT department who will act as the guide. The trap for the business users is that they want to order cloud services themselves. Cloud can be so appealing and easy at first glance that they might think they do not need the internal IT department anymore. The result is that the business user will end up in a mess: a bunch of services that are not integrated but cannot easily be discarded will cause the business to be locked into inefficient provisioning. In the end, the expected benefits are nullified. Like any other investment, the cloud can generate benefits but it also has its costs.

When creating a business case for cloud computing, the benefits and costs shown in Table 4.1 should be taken into consideration.

Potential benefits of cloud computing	Potential costs of cloud computing
Improved agility: IT solutions respond faster to changing business needs	Migration costs: costs to migrate a current solution to a cloud service
Improved time-to-operations: ready to quickly get something up and running to meet new business needs	Switching costs: costs to switch from the chosen provider to another provider
Cost reduction: decrease in all types of costs associated with building and running internal IT	Integration costs: costs to make the cloud services work together with current business processes, applications, and infrastructure
Risk reduction: decrease in risks of running internal IT, such as business continuity	Implementation costs: costs to prepare employees for the change, embed the change and educate employees
Increased revenue: improved sales resulting from entering new markets or using new business models	Costs of increased risks: what are the costs associated with increased risks, such as data security?

Table 4.1: Benefits and costs of cloud computing

> Booz, Allen, Hamilton has conducted an economic analysis to investigate the potential savings of cloud computing for the US government. They concluded that, over a 13-year life cycle, the total cost of implementing and sustaining a cloud environment may be as much as two-thirds lower than maintaining a traditional, non-virtualized IT data centre. It should be noted that this requires a transition and implementation that will take several years (Alford and Morton 2010).

In any case, the business user is expected to drive the change: find business opportunities, engage the internal IT department and expect them to act as a business in providing services from a service catalogue, just like cloud providers.

Internal IT department as the broker

As stated before, the internal IT department will increasingly be compared with external service providers like the cloud providers who sell hardware and software as a service priced per use. This is a threat for most internal IT departments, because they are often not yet able to offer services. And even when they are offering comparable services, they are not able to match the pricepoint of external providers. So the internal IT department is under pressure.

On the other hand, the internal IT department has a much deeper under-standing of its business users, of the IT market and the organization's hard-ware and software landscape than external providers. In addition, somebody in the organization has to look after integration, safeguard the corporate risks and try to achieve purchasing synergies.

The internal IT department is in the best position to deal with these threats and opportunities, and to buy, integrate and orchestrate services. The internal IT department effectively becomes an intermediary between the internal customer and all internal and external service providers.

As well as performing a broker function, most large internal IT departments will use cloud technology to provide their internal customers with private cloud services. The challenge for IT is to develop the right mix of internal and external capabilities in order to become a best-in-class service provider for their internal customers.

Incumbent service providers can build on customer relationships

These providers traditionally have strong relationships with their clients. They can build on these relationships to help their customers implement cloud services. On the other hand, they can consume cloud services them-selves and integrate these in their service offerings (for example, for develop-ment and testing). They can even act as a cloud broker between their custom-ers and cloud providers. They know their clients and the IT market very well and, due to their large scale, are able to buy cloud services for the best price and resell or package these services to their clients. They can also offer man-aged access to different kinds of cloud services. This might be attractive for these clients who have neither the scale nor the capability to explore the IT market.

Because of cloud computing, service providers taking on the role of producer can now provide a larger set of services to their clients and gain a bigger share of the total expenditure by these clients. Of course they will meet with some pressure due to their business model, because these services will be delivered on a subscription basis instead of an hourly fee basis.

Incumbent service providers invest in cloud computing because they face a growing demand from their clients for help in adopting cloud computing and rolling it out across their organizations. Typical services they develop are cloud adoption roadmaps and cloud maturity models.

IBM, for example, developed a whole range of services based on the idea of a hybrid cloud, extending the enterprise perimeter to the cloud (Boulton 2010).

Software providers have to rethink their business model

This is the area where a lot is happening. Traditional software providers are under extreme pressure to rethink their business model. The existing license model is rapidly being replaced by a subscription model. Another challenge for the traditional software providers is to change the level of granularity of their services. Their current software has often a very low level of granularity, too low to determine the match between the needed functionality for a given business process and the services. Most ERP-systems are still monolithic and far from being service-oriented.

The main ERP vendors SAP and Oracle, who sell their software through licenses, face strong competition from new players like Salesforce in the CRM area. Salesforce is providing CRM as a service via the subscription model.

Similar competition takes place in the market for generic applications like email and office software. Microsoft, relying on the license model, was and still is the dominant player in this market but is now facing competition from Google, who uses the subscription model. Google is now able to offer an email solution in the cloud for a fixed and relative low cost per user. Microsoft, realizing it has a lot to lose, has concluded that they must be able to offer their software via the subscription model, too. They now invest heavily in cloud.

About 70% of their 40,000 developers are working on cloud developments either directly or indirectly. As Steve Balmer said: "for the cloud, we're all in." (Dubie 2010).

Hardware providers face a shift in demand

Traditionally, hardware is bought or leased by the internal IT department. In the cloud era hardware is either sold as a service or incorporated into other services, just like software.

Hardware providers like HP, IBM and Dell face competition from Amazon who offers infrastructure as a service through the cloud. In response the traditional market leaders will have to find ways to do exactly the same.

The fact that software is provided as a service implies that hardware providers will see an increased demand from cloud service providers. Microsoft, Google, Amazon, IBM and the like are buying a lot of hardware to build huge data centers to provide cloud services around the world. The internal IT department, on the contrary, will buy less hardware.

It is still unclear whether cloud computing will reduce the total capacity of computer hardware required worldwide. It is expected that cloud computing will increase the average utilization level dramatically. On the other hand, the availability of clouds will drive new ways of using computer capacity, such as for analytics, which could offset the gains from efficiency.

Cloud providers set the pace

Companies like Amazon Web Services, Google and Salesforce are already providing cloud services on a pay-per-use fee—sometimes even for free.

Amazon Web Services (AWS) offers a highly standardized commodity platform via a subscription model. AWS was one of the first real cloud providers. The story goes that Amazon introduced their Elastic Compute Cloud (EC2) because they developed a highly available and scalable infrastructure for their retail business that was only in demand during the Christmas season, not for the rest of the year. By re-using this spare capacity for other purposes, Amazon was building on the same core capabilities they had to develop for their retail business. On the other hand, it was largely by coincidence that Amazon jumped into the cloud business. One of their lead developers, Chris Pinkham, got homesick and wanted to go back to his home in South Africa. Because Amazon didn't want him to leave the company, they gave him the freedom to innovate. As a result, EC2 was born in 2006 (Higginbotham 2010). Cloud computing is just another business model for Amazon, but it is a fast-growing one. It is estimated that cloud services could generate about $650 million in sales for AWS in 2010.

Google is offering cloud services like Gmail, Google Apps and Picasa. These are geared to consumers and small- and medium-sized enterprises. Most of their services are free, at least for consumers. Because Google is able to attract a lot of people to their services they can attract a lot of advertisements. These advertisements are their main revenue stream. Google is also active in the market for large enterprises with cloud services like Google Apps (Bradshaw 2010).

Companies like Amazon, Google and Salesforce definitely set the pace. They are closely watched by all other service providers.

And new providers are entering the market by offering cloud services specific to certain communities, like government. In Chapter 8, we will discuss the role of government in the context of cloud computing and data.

4.5 Conclusion

The bottom line of this chapter is that cloud computing has a significant impact on IT economics. The way IT services are produced, distributed, consumed and charged will change dramatically. The subscription model where hardware and software is sold as a service is quite different from traditional models where licenses, hours and hardware components were sold. This again has an impact on the way the business users are charged by IT. Billing becomes much more transparent. The business gets insight into what it is paying for. This influences their buying behavior, and certainly has a positive influence on the business-IT relationship. At the end of the day, the overall benefits to business might be considerable!

For the IT parties involved, the question remains who will be ready to benefit and who will have a hard time to adjust. The internal IT department will face strong competition from cloud providers and has to rethink its role, most likely changing from a supplier of services to a broker of services. The incumbent service providers have a different opportunity: to help their customers with cloud computing. On the other hand the self service aspect of cloud computing will put some pressure on the demand for these providers. The software providers are under the largest pressure. They face strong competition from the cloud providers and are rethinking not just their pricing, but their entire business model. Some of these software providers will start to offer their solutions as a service, others may being too reluctant or slow to adapt and could lose marketshare dramatically. Finally hardware providers will see a change in their client base. Instead of the internal IT departments, providers of cloud services will become their prime customers, probably asking for different products that better fit the cloud datacenters.

In the next chapter we will discuss in more depth the changing role for the internal IT department.

Dutch Government Familiarizing Itself With All of Its Cloud Options
Clear Benefits of Cloud Don't Obscure Need to Do Homework

On its surface, cloud computing is a no-brainer. It's a model for delivering corporate technology in a way that contains costs, reduces the environmental footprint of data centers, and makes powerful business applications readily available on an anytime, anywhere basis. But that doesn't mean there aren't significant considerations, such as security and privacy, that an organization should take into account when looking to transition to the cloud.

This is why the government of The Netherlands is being careful to perform due diligence before proceeding with plans to introduce cloud computing into its environment. ICTU, the Dutch agency that oversees the implementation of information and communications technologies, is currently investigating cloud computing, and determining its potential role in delivering E-government.

Since early 2010, ICTU has been turning over every rock—from researching vendors to analyzing legal risks—in an effort to fully understand what its cloud computing options are, get a handle on the associated costs, set realistic expectations, and make sure that the potential business implications of moving into the cloud are perfectly clear. The effort, says ICTU advisor Paul Suijkerbuijk, has been spurred by two things: the desire to lower data center costs, and a steady stream of suggestions from vendors that it's time for the Dutch government to consider cloud computing.

Cloud Dovetails Nicely With Dutch Government's Goals

The cloud also has become a more interesting option because of ICTU's efforts on another front: It's rebuilding the Dutch government's main web site, which will make it easier for citizenry to log in and access personal information, as well as more general information about nationwide services. And it's approaching the site modularly, developing building blocks—such as storage and search—that can easily be combined in an interoperable cloud environment. A cloud-enabled E-government site would simplify the delivery of a wide range of applications available as subscription-based services, thus reducing ICTU's development workload.

That's not all. Suijkerbuijk says that in the future the cloud also could be used to deliver business applications to civil servants, as well as to run some of the primary business process environments on which governmental departments rely. The cloud strategy, once adopted, is likely to start with the E-government initiative, then move on to civil servant computing resources before tackling the more unwieldy business process environments. "The bigger the system you have to move into the cloud, the more difficult it is," he says.

Establishing a greener IT operation that minimizes power and cooling needs also is a factor, although Suijkerbuijk says that it's proving difficult to quantify the real gains organizations realize in this area as they move from traditional hosting models to the cloud.

European Privacy Protections Always Lurking

But all of these things take a back seat initially to another consideration: Unlike organizations in America that have been moving full-steam-ahead on cloud deployments, ICTU and other European entities exploring the cloud face a unique set of privacy-related challenges.

"In the U.S., it's easier to put something in the cloud," says Suijkerbuijk. "American companies are hosting these clouds, and it's quite obvious that data stored in the cloud is also in America. These same companies are offering their services in Europe, storing data in the U.S, and we're not allowed to store governmental or personal data in foreign countries."

As a result, ICTU is exploring the possibility of spearheading government-wide cloud efforts that would store data within the boundaries of The Netherlands, enabling it to make something like Google Docs available to Dutch government workers. If that proves impossible, there's a chance ICTU could find itself developing a similar type of productivity application suite itself, as there is no Dutch equivalent to Google Docs.

The idea of a government-wide cloud, or of an ICTU-built version of Google Docs, speaks directly to what Suijkerbuijk believes is one of the greatest opportunities to put the cloud into action in The Netherlands: namely, working together. Many Dutch governmental entities, including 400 cities, are investigating cloud computing, and while none are obliged to be part of a standardized government cloud, a joint effort would help everyone, Suijkerbuijk says.

Innovation Centre to Encourage Focus on Cloud Applications

In lieu of that cooperation, Suijkerbuijk has some advice for other Dutch organizations trying to justify cloud investments. He suggests that instead of focusing on the anticipated cost savings and environmental improvements, they should look at the expected impact on application development and functionality, which could be even more dramatic. This also speaks more to the inevitability of the cloud; it's not so much a matter of whether the Dutch government will move into the cloud, but rather how far.

That inevitability is why Suijkerbuijk's focus has been on heading up development of a cloud computing innovation centre that's expected to be operational by the end of 2010. The center will serve as a cloud testing environment where Dutch agencies can try out applications and get help with their first steps into the cloud.

Once the innovation centre is open, says Suijkerbuijk, "We will start developing building blocks and offer cloud services as soon as possible."

When Building Cloud Applications, Target Market's Limitations Must Be Considered
Investment-Matching Service Provides Template for Complex Cloud Apps

Building applications that will reside in the cloud—particularly complex commercial applications that will be sold to financial services companies—requires some careful consideration. With questions lingering about the cloud's readiness to satisfy the financial services industry's stringent requirements in the areas of security, reliability and performance, it's critical that software-as-a-service offerings be built with these perceived limitations in mind.

That's exactly how Laurentiu Vasiliu focused his team's energy in building the suite of services his startup company, Peracton Ltd., launched earlier this year. Those services—based on algorithms Vasiliu and his team helped write while on staff at the National University of Ireland Galway's Digital Enterprise Research Institute—are able to identify the mutual funds that best fit a customer's investment profile in a matter of seconds.

The idea behind Peracton's service is two-fold. It speeds up the process of determining the best investment vehicles for a financial customer, thus replacing a manual process that has involved using Excel spreadsheets to categorize thousands of mutual funds, each conforming to more than 20 investment parameters. It also is designed to show, with mathematical precision, exactly why a particular fund was chosen, an important consideration in a highly regulated industry.

As tricky as the application sounds, building it as a cloud service made things even trickier. It had to work across vast geographies and networks as if it were running on a server in the next room—something Vasiliu demonstrated in a demo for customers on both coasts of the U.S. while he was in North Africa and the software was running on servers in Ireland.

Application Tweaks Provide Valuable Lessons

Not surprisingly, Vasiliu has emerged from the experience of developing the service with some pretty clear ideas of things software designers need to consider when building cloud-based applications.

Peracton's work to make the technology cloud-compliant started with the graphic user interface. Vasiliu knew the tendency of developers is to build applications

73

that look great, but he decided his team should take a different approach, keeping the interface basic so as not to have the network get bogged down trying to serve up snazzy images and design elements. "If the graphic interface looks great but is slow, what's the point?" asks Vasiliu.

The next issue was configurability, a crucial element of a service that would be sold primarily as a "white label" component of a service integrator's integrated solution. Highly configurable cloud applications can require that as much as 60 percent of the software be reworked in order to achieve desired configurations. Vasiliu wanted Peracton's service to lower the burden on IT teams by ensuring that re-configurations only require reworking 5 percent to 10 percent of the core software.

Then, of course, there was the matter of addressing the admittedly stringent security requirements of a target market of institutional customers that may not yet be confident about exchanging sensitive financial data in the cloud. Vasiliu and his team made sure their software was designed to work with the most popular and accepted security system protocols. But during the design, when it became clear that the embedded security schemes for protecting transmitted data might not meet the requirements of some institutions, the service was tweaked to enable it to tap the most popular protocols for negotiating firewalls, as well.

App's Market Message Intended to Reflect Industry's Cloud Sentiments

Even with the interface, configurability and security addressed, Vasiliu is well aware that he's still dealing with what is perhaps the most cloud-averse industry. Despite financial services companies' growing comfort with packaged integrator offerings that feature white label services such as Peracton's, Vasiliu still has chosen to exercise caution when using the "cloud computing" terminology of which financial services executives are so wary.

"Even though our software is in the cloud, I'm careful not to use the buzzwords, and instead say we have a web-based application," he says. In fact, Peracton's service is available in both cloud-based and on-premise versions.

For the short term, Vasiliu expects to have to dance around the topic of the cloud while the industry continues getting accustomed to the idea of placing data-intensive apps in the cloud. But he's confident that as developers grow savvier about what financial services companies require from cloud services, and as network capacity increases, the uncertainty Peracton encounters in the market today will fall away. "In five to seven years," Vasiliu says, "the path to the cloud will get clearer."

5 The New IT Constitution

5.1 Introduction

The cloud offers a new way to consume and deliver IT resources, so it is logical to ask what the impact of the cloud will be on the way IT is managed and how it relates to the core business. In this chapter we will argue that a "new IT constitution" is required for the enterprise to gain real benefits from cloud computing. These benefits cannot be fully realized simply by implementing a technical solution, such as a cloud management platform, or purely by consuming services from an external provider through a public cloud. Changes to IT governance, management capabilities and processes are needed—hence, a new IT constitution. Some recent cloud implementation projects have devoted up to 50 percent of the total effort to these issues. Enterprises who have ignored the need for IT management and process changes, and focused simply on the technical implementation of cloud, may fail to realize net benefits.

Examples of cloud computing cases where it would have been better if changes in IT management and processes had been included upfront:

Cloud service consumption
A line-of-business unit in an organization procures public cloud services without going through the organization's internal IT department. Costs are incurred with the public provider. Unless there is a corresponding reduction in costs within the internal IT department, the cloud procurement has resulted in increasing the total cost to the organization.

Cloud service delivery
An internal IT department implements a cloud management platform on top of their virtualized infrastructure, with the resource pool consisting of previously allocated projects and services. When the business wants to add on a new service, they still need to procure resources for the cloud pool in the traditional method: by signing a purchase order, waiting for the vendor to deliver the physical equipment, and hoping the IT department will rack it and stack it quickly, so that it can be used in the cloud. In this scenario, not all the benefits of cloud services are being realized, since the

> processes to manage the capacity and the resource pool separately from the delivery process have not been considered.

In this chapter we consider the main drivers for a new IT constitution. We identify some critical new IT capabilities that the cloud will demand, and suggest some tools to analyze current IT management capabilities and processes to determine what needs to change.

5.2 Drivers for the New IT Constitution

Cloud enables "self-service" IT

The concept of "self service" is at the core of cloud computing. Just like the PC did in the 1980s, the cloud, and especially the public cloud, enables department-level business managers to procure their own IT systems. They can declare independence from corporate IT with its long planning cycles, slow response times and rationed resources. Across many enterprises, Line-of-Business (LoB) departments are already procuring cloud services independent from IT. The rise of Salesforce.com is a major example of this trend. In 2010 Gartner estimated that Salesforce.com had gained market share to hold 12,5 percent of the CRM market, placing it third in the list of CRM vendors after SAP and Oracle (Shread 2010).

While many business executives may welcome this opportunity to break free from the shackles of IT, there are real risks to the business. To continue the analogy with the PC revolution, the explosion in "do it yourself" IT with managers running the business on spreadsheets led to a massive explosion in unmanaged data and a whole generation of new problems relating to security, data integrity and auditing that still plague many organizations.

Cloud services pose similar risks, as well as some new ones, since the data is now outside the enterprise firewall. For example, the marketing department of a large consumer services company decided to use a third-party marketing database for managing campaigns. Fairly soon the data in the third-party database fell out of sync with the company's master customer data, resulting in incorrect mailings and reduced customer satisfaction.

But essentially the dynamic is the same: on the one hand, self-service IT promises flexibility and responsiveness, while on the other hand, centralized IT promises control and efficiency.

Self service, of course, implies that the business users take responsibility for aspects of IT that were previously handled by the IT department. Many business users are probably not aware of the background administration tasks that they may have unwittingly taken on by opting for a cloud service. Backups and security patching are two obvious examples. As cloud evolves, it is likely that these will be offered as "value added" services by the public cloud-service providers, but IT leaders need to make sure their users understand the risks and responsibilities of self-service computing.

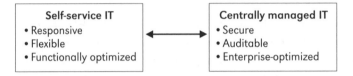

Figure 5.1: The traditional IT dilemma

Innovation will come from outside the firewall

One of the great benefits of the Internet age is that enterprises enjoy much greater access to market innovation. Successful and agile enterprises will want to exploit innovative new technologies and solutions wherever they are found, and embed them into their business processes. Cloud is a great enabler, as it allows businesses to adopt new tools and processes much more rapidly and flexibly than before. Gone is the dependency on IT departments to identify, plan and implement innovative new business tools, since they can now be picked up in the global market. This calls into question traditional ways of doing IT strategy that assume internal IT will be the main engine of business process innovation.

External cloud services provide a lower entry cost and a relatively low-risk way for businesses to experiment with new business concepts and IT solutions.

Non-value-added functions are being relentlessly commoditized

As discussed in Chapter 4, chargeback and market-price comparison will force IT departments to constantly justify the cost of their services. It is likely that this will be increasingly hard for non-differentiating functions that have been commoditized, such as email. The cloud offers a more liquid market for such commodity services, which in turn will drive down costs. IT departments will need to identify which business functions are core and differentiating, and which ones are non-core and commodity. Then they can plan to exploit commodity cloud services wherever it makes sense, in order to drive down costs.

Service orientation comes of age

Many IT departments have been on an SOA journey for several years now. Although some SOA programs have become mostly a software engineering exercise, with a focus on SOA as a programming model, the promise of service orientation to provide reusable, flexible, dynamic, loosely coupled components to enable dynamic business processes remains real, and truly comes of age with cloud and the concept of "anything-as-a-service."

An essential characteristic of the cloud is that it formalizes a service contract between service consumer and service provider. The abstraction of the cloud service means that the consumer is isolated from decisions about how or where the cloud service is delivered. The service contract specifies service characteristics like availability, performance, security and functionality in terms that can be understood by the business user.

This is in fact a generalization of the concept of service orientation. From being merely about software modules and interfaces, services can now be provided at any level of the stack: storage services up to software-as-a-service.

It's important here to distinguish between a business service and an IT service. What businesses want to buy "as a service" is typically a business function, which is typically expressed in business terms such as "customer management." This typically breaks down into a set of lower-level business processes (enroll a customer, manage a sales campaign), which are sufficiently granular to be defined precisely enough to implement "as a service"

with SLAs, service contracts, *etc.* What IT provides in terms of a service catalogue is often a much lower-level set of IT functions (deploy a workstation,
enroll a user, deploy a server). Therefore, there must be service catalogues at
multiple levels, with around 20-30 offerings in the high-level business service
catalogue and several hundred in the detailed IT service catalogue.

We should also note that the concept of a service is key to Information Technology Infrastructure Library (ITIL) V3. We touch on the relationship between
ITIL and cloud services later in this chapter.

While the notion of "anything-as-a-service" embodies the principle of service
orientation at a theoretical level, there are many additional requirements for
cloud services to be truly "service oriented" as a SOA practitioner would
understand it. For example, there should be clear service protocols and standards to identify, instantiate, use and terminate a service, or clearly defined
use cases and service behaviors. Many cloud services today are not constructed with a standard and structured service interface. Cloud standards,
such as those being developed by the Distributed Management Task Force
(see DMTF in the References section of this book) and the Open Group Cloud
Work Group (see The Open Group in the References section of this book) will
become essential.

Integration remains the watchword

All of the above trends reinforce the need for IT to act as an integrator of
external and internally provided services. Rather than focus on the content
of these services, the role of IT is more to focus on the ability to assemble and
disassemble them into new business processes. We might use the term
"orchestrator" to define this role. This requires several levels of integration.
At the infrastructure level, IT needs to provide key service management capabilities to provision, monitor and secure these services regardless of where
they are delivered from. IT must provide integrated service delivery.

At the platform level, IT needs to integrate applications and data to ensure
consistency of data across multiple applications: both internal and in the
cloud. And finally, at the business process level, there is a need to integrate
the business events and data managed by these applications in the context of
integrated business processes.

These integration disciplines are not new, and IT has been delivering tools and approaches to achieving integration for many years. What cloud brings is a new dimension: the need to integrate services, some of which may be delivered by external service providers over whom IT has no control and which are inherently dynamic. New tools are emerging that address these new aspects of cloud integration, such as RightScale for cloud management (see RightScale in the References section of this book) and IBM's Cast Iron (Cast Iron 2010) for application and data integration.

5.3 New IT Capabilities for the Cloud Era

The drivers discussed above will affect different IT departments in different ways, and to different levels. We propose that there are three capabilities of IT management that will assume increasing importance as IT transitions into the cloud era.

What are these three capabilities?

IT as orchestrator of services

The concept of business technology (BT) introduces the idea that IT must separate the functions of "IT business enablement" from "IT operational excellence" (Cameron 2009). This separation allows IT to become a broker of external services as well as one of the main providers of services to the business. In essence, a new IT "supply chain" is established, as illustrated in Figure 5.2.

In this model, the broker function manages the service catalogue and works with business to select appropriate IT services from the catalogue. It also has the role of managing the business process aspects of orchestration—ensuring that all the services knit together to support the business needs.

The internal provider function is responsible for the secure, safe, and efficient delivery of internal IT services—whether delivered using traditional "siloed" IT systems or based on private cloud technology. In addition, it works with the broker function on orchestration, focusing on the service delivery, information integrity, management and compliance aspects of managing multiple cloud

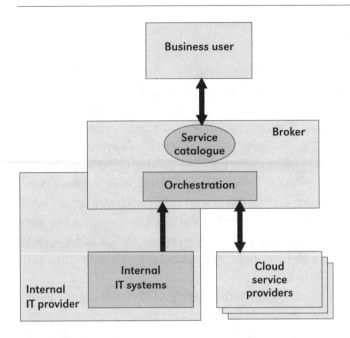

Figure 5.2: New IT supply chain

providers. These providers will operate at all levels—software, platform and infrastructure as a service—and some may be suppliers to the internal IT function.

Later in this chapter we discuss how existing service management frameworks, such as ITIL, can be used to analyze the changes to the IT service management processes that are required to allow this "orchestrator" role to deliver integrated service management across internal and external service providers.

IT as venture capitalist

An important aspect of the 'business excellence' role of IT is to manage the portfolio of business services that are available within the service catalogue. The model here is that of a "venture capitalist"—IT builds a complementary and dynamic portfolio of services selected for their functional excellence, innovation, service excellence and cost characteristics. Managing this portfolio is a new IT capability that goes beyond traditional supplier management.

IT as app store provider

The massive success of the Apple iPhone and its "app store" model has led many IT leaders to consider its applicability to enterprise IT services. Apple even launched the "Mac App Store" with apps for their Mac computers (Weiss 2010). The UK government's G-cloud program is a major exponent of this approach (Espiner 2009). The G-cloud is intended to include an app store where government and local government agencies can purchase software and services from a variety of providers. They will be able to access software demonstrations, work out implementation costs, and order software on an automated basis, both in standard commercial packages and bespoke software applications. The app store will also include components such as a payment object for money transfer, which could be embedded into multiple suites.

The app store model is particularly appealing to large, federated organizations (such as governments) as a means of harmonizing software acquisition and deployment across multiple user departments. It would be implemented from a technical perspective using the service catalogue.

One approach to building an enterprise app store is to give the business freedom to provision their own tools, subject to guidelines, and after gaining some experience, to standardize on one variation. For example, if everybody starts to use a certain project-management tool in the cloud, then the enterprise can negotiate a better deal with that provider. From then on, that becomes the mandatory choice for their PM tools.

5.4 Mapping the New IT Capabilities for the Cloud

Given that these new capabilities are needed, delivering them will have a significant impact on the IT management processes and organization. Enterprises need a map of IT capabilities that can help to identify what needs to change or improve for the adoption of cloud services. Two such maps are Forrester Research's "IT Capability Map" (Scott 2010) and IBM's "Component Business Model" (Pohle *et al.* 2005). Both Forrester and IBM have developed general business mapping tools that have been used to map the capabilities of the IT function itself. In the next section we consider in more detail how to use IBM's Component Business Model to analyze the impact of the cloud on IT processes and capabilities.

Using the Component Business Model to analyze the impact of the cloud on IT processes and capabilities

This section describes the IBM Component Business Model for IT as a framework for understanding which processes will be impacted by a cloud solution.

Cloud computing touches many sectors within an organization to a greater or lesser extent. The impact of cloud-service consumption is very different from the impact of cloud-service provision. Each and every organization is unique in how it differentiates itself and adds value to the goods and services that drive its revenue, and in the implementation of business processes that make up command and control within the organization. Within whole industries, many of the business processes have become standardized as best practices, but the implementation of these processes in terms of policy, procedures and standards remains truly unique. In order to assess which processes are impacted by cloud services, and to what extent, we need a framework to map the processes and represent the organization.

> **What is a component business model?**
> IBM uses component business models as a method for representing the entire business in a simple framework that fits on a single page. It is an evolution of traditional views of a business, such as business unit, function, location or process. Using the component business model, it is possible to identify the basic building blocks of the business. Each building block includes the people, processes and technology needed by this component to act as a standalone entity and deliver value to the organization.
> The Component Business Map (CBM) shows activities across lines of business, without the constrictions of locations, internal silos or business units. The Component Business Map shows the entire company on a single page, making it extremely easy to visualize the impact of a particular initiative: in this context, cloud computing.
> As shown in Figure 5.3, the top row, "direct," represents all of those components in the business that set the overall strategy and direction for the organization. The middle row, "control," represents all of the components in the business that translate those plans into actions, in addition to managing the day-to-day running of those activities. The bottom row, "execute," contains the business components that actually execute the detailed activities and plans of the organization.
> Each CBM is unique to each company: the columns are created after thorough analysis of a business's functions and value chain, and the rows are defined by actions.

However, the anchor point for each CBM is an industry model selected to represent a close starting point for each organization. Figure 5.3 shows a sample CBM from the retail industry. The columns represent the business process categories/groups. The intersection of the rows and columns contains the processes.

	Customers	Products/ Services	Channels	Logistics	Business Administration
Direct	Market Strategy	Merchandise Planning	Channel Strategy	Network Design	Corporate Strategy
		Channel Planning	Store Design		Corporate Planning
	Customer Service Strategy	Assortment Planning	Real Estate Strategy	Warehouse Design	
		Space Planning	Internet Design		Financial Planning
	Marketing Strategy	Promotion Planning	Catalog & Call Center Design	Demand/Flow Planning	Corporate Governance
		Product Planning			
		Sourcing			
Control	Campaign Mgt	Product Flow	Channel Mgt	Inbound Routing	Budget Performance Mgt
		Planogramming			
		Allocation	Order Mgt	Receipt Scheduling	Treasury & Risk Mgt
		Inventory Mgt			
	Service Mgt	Demand Forecast	Labor Mgt	Delivery Scheduling	Legal & Regulatory Compliance
		Price Management			
		Content Mgt	Facilities Mgt	Carrier Mgt	Inventory Control
		Vendor Mgt			
Execute	Customer Service	Item Mgt	Order Mgt	Warehouse Mgt	Financial Reporting & Accounting
	Customer Communications	Product Mgt	Inventory Mgt	Transportation Mgt	Indirect Procurement
		PO Mgt			
	Marketing	Vendor Mgt	Merchandise Mgt	Fleet Mgt	HR Administration
	Advertising	Replenishment			
	Public Relations	Revenue/Clearance Mgt	Price/Sign Mgt	Reverse Logistics	IT Systems & Operations

Figure 5.3: Sample CBM from the retail industry (copyright 2010 IBM Corporation)

Impact of cloud computing on the business of IT

To analyze the impact of cloud computing, we use the CBM for the "business of IT"—which applies to service providers or internal IT organizations. Figure 5.4 shows the raw CBM for the "business of IT".

	IT Customer Relationship	IT Business Strategy	IT Business Administration	Business Resilience	Information	Service&Solution Development	Service&Solution Deployment	Service&Solution Support
Direct	Customer Business Intelligence; Customer Transformation Needs Identification	Business Techn & Strategy Govern; Portfolio Strategy Mgt; Enterprise Architecture; Service Mgt Strategy	IT Business Model	Business Risk & Compliance Strategy; Business Resilience Strategy	Information Strategy	Development Strategy	Deployment Strategy	Service Delivery Strategy; Service Support Strategy
Control	Market Planning & Communications; Customer Transformation Consulting & Guidance; Service Demand & Performance Planning	IT Management System Control; Portfolio Value Mgt; Technology Innovation	Financial Control & Accounting; Site & Facility Administration; HR Planning & Administration; Sourcing Relationships & Selection	Business Risk & Compliance Control; Continuous Business Operations Planning; Security, Privacy & Data Protection	Information Architecture; Information Lifecycle Planning & Control	Service & Solution Lifecycle Planning; Service & Solution Architecture	Service & Solution Implementation Planning; Change Deployment Control	Service Delivery Control; Infrastructure Resource Planning; Service Support Planning
Execute	Service & Solution Selling; Service Performance Analysis	Project Mgt; Knowledge Mgt	Procurement & Contracts; Vendor Service Coordination; Customer Contracts & Pricing	Business Compliance Analysis; Business Resilience Operations; User Identity & Access Processing	Information Content	Service & Solution Creation & Testing; Service & Solution Maintenance & Testing	Technology Implementation; Service & Solution Rollout	Service Delivery Operations; Infrastructure Resource Operations; Service Support Operations

Figure 5.4: "Business of IT" CBM (copyright 2010 IBM Corporation)

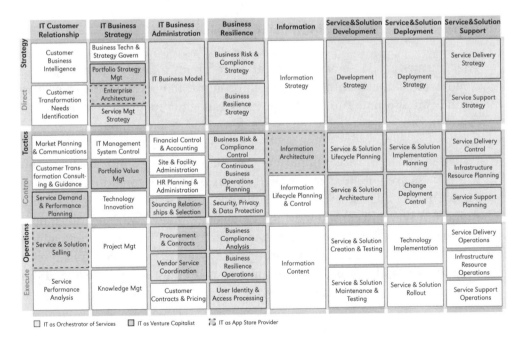

Figure 5.5: Mapping new IT capabilities on the "business of IT" CBM (copyright 2010 IBM Corporation)

The new IT capabilities described above (IT as orchestrator of services, IT as venture capitalist and IT as app store provider) can be mapped to this model in the form of a "heat map," which shows the impact on the IT department of acquiring these capabilities. One potential heat map is shown in Figure 5.5.

In this analysis, it can be seen that the IT as venture capitalist capability affects primarily IT business strategy and IT business administration functions—at all levels. An enterprise app store primarily impacts upon architecture: both enterprise architecture and information architecture, but also on the "selling" of IT services. Orchestrator of services capability is more pervasive, and has a strong impact on the tactical and strategic aspects of service development, deployment and support. There is less impact potentially at lower levels, since these operational aspects are typically existing IT processes for "in house" services, or are outsourced to a service provider.

The mapping shown in Figure 5.5 is intended to be illustrative and not definitive. Each organization's heat map will be different depending on their current organizational maturity, capabilities and strategy. The CBM model provides a framework for analysis, not a definitive solution.

Impact of the private cloud on the business of IT

The "business of IT" model can be used to produce heat maps for specific cloud implementation projects. If we consider the impact of creating a private cloud in an internal IT organization, it's possible to produce a heat map indicating the areas most impacted by the new cloud delivery models.

Figure 5.6 shows the areas impacted when implementing a private cloud. The white areas are not impacted at all. It's clear that cloud computing, as a new service delivery model, will have a profound impact upon the deployment and support of IT services. Likewise, the IT business model will need to change to implement pay-per-use pricing, and capacity planning will have to adjust to the implications of scale-up as well as scale-down. By drawing a heat map using the CBM, the priorities in optimizing processes become clear, and the scale of effort can begin to be gauged.

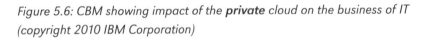

Figure 5.6: CBM showing impact of the **private** cloud on the business of IT (copyright 2010 IBM Corporation)

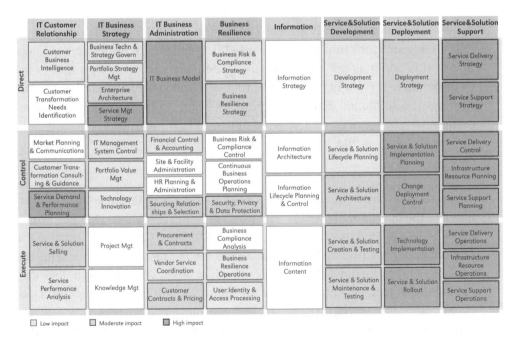

Figure 5.7: CBM showing the impact of **public** cloud services on the business of IT (copyright 2010 IBM Corporation)

Impact of the public cloud on the business of IT

It is likely that a heat map for a public cloud implementation (see Figure 5.7) will touch on many more areas than a private cloud, as the public cloud services will be more fundamental to the organization's core business. It's not unexpected that security and privacy experience increased impact, as do the business resilience strategy and operations.

So by using a process framework (like CBM) and heat map analysis, the process optimization requirements can be assessed and a corrective action plan developed.

5.5 The Cloud and Service Management— ITIL and the Cloud

The CBM heat map analysis for cloud services shows clearly that service management is the area most impacted by the cloud. So a more in-depth analysis of the impact of the cloud on service management processes will be needed.

A very common and widely adopted approach for IT service management is ITIL®. Organizations that have adopted ITIL (see ITIL in the References section of this book) as the basis for service delivery can use it as a tool to re-examine their service management processes and governance in light of the new operating model that cloud requires—especially the role of IT as an orchestrator of services, as discussed above. ITIL V3 with its service orientation is suitable as the basis for planning the service delivery aspects of cloud.

When services are delivered by the cloud, it impacts both the technical solution and the operational process. The way a solution is realized changes, which needs to be directed by enterprise architects (see also Chapter 6). But also the responsibility for operational processes, their character or nature, and the methods of service delivery and control will change. This means that service management is highly impacted by the cloud. Due to the dynamic nature of cloud computing, service portfolios become more changeable, which at the same time leads to the existence of more underpinning contracts. Services from different providers and of different natures need to be presented to the business as a consistent set. Incident, problem and change management needs to be carried out in different forms, depending on the nature of the cloud services and the underlying service level agreements, to name a few very striking examples of the cloud's impact on service management. Cloud computing requires a higher maturity in most of the service management areas than we have ever seen before.

ITIL is a library of best practices that provides a practical, no-nonsense framework for identifying, planning, delivering and supporting IT services to the business. When moving to the cloud, it is advisable to (re)deploy ITIL processes. In many organizations that have already adopted ITIL, processes have become rigid and bureaucratic over time. The journey to the cloud is an excellent opportunity to dust off these processes and improve service management. If ITIL is not already in use, it's the appropriate time to consider implementing it to face cloud challenges in the service management area.

ITIL is a huge library, so implementing or redeploying/redesigning it as a whole isn't a feasible strategy. In order to support cloud computing, Table 5.1 highlights the areas and processes to focus on. The last column of the table illustrates the minimum requirements for service management. At least these ITIL processes have to be changed to be able to act as a provider of cloud services.

Maturity of service management is a key success factor in implementing cloud services. Keeping service management in step with cloud computing initiatives is imperative, so involving service managers (and consequently, operations) is an important issue.

ITIL main area	ITIL process	Required change by cloud computing	At a minimum required
Service Strategy	Service Portfolio Management	Make sure to present an integrated service portfolio to end-users, independent of service realization	
	Financial Management	Introduce new pricing models to provide flexible pricing (such as pay per use)	√
Service Design	Service Catalogue Management	(re)Deploy a service catalogue with standardized services, (re)defined in business terms, avoiding technical implementation details. This should be done in close cooperation with (enterprise) architects, who define solution patterns and standards	√

ITIL main area	ITIL process	Required change by cloud computing	At a minimum required
	Service Level Management	Define SLA's which are set up per service per customer	√
	Capacity Management	Implement a capacity forecasting model which can take into account the characteristics of cloud related services	√
	IT Service Continuity Management	Ensure service operation continuity; distributed implementation of solutions (at different cloud providers) can put continuity at risk, if not guarded carefully	
Service Transition	Change Management	Redefine change management processes according to the changes in responsibility and consider automating these processes to support the rapid provisioning of cloud related services	√
	Service Asset & Configuration Management	Automated discovery for real time information, as only a portion of the service chain can be stored (as static information) in the configuration management system	√
	Service Validation and Testing	Ensure proper operation and integration of (cloud) services in the IT-landscape	
Service Operations	Event & Incident Management	Align service desks with cloud providers event & incident management processes. Consider tooling to manage and meter a highly automated environment	√
	Request Fulfillment	Consider a self enablement portal	√
	Problem Management	Agree on problem management processes with cloud providers in order to be able to trace and solve problems (root cause analyses)	
Continual Service Improvement	Service Measurement	Ensure that end-users have a consistent service quality experience, independent of implementation	

Table 5.1: Areas in ITIL to focus on to support cloud computing

5.6 **Conclusion**

In this chapter we've considered the IT capability and process changes that cloud computing will drive. We identified a number of specific drivers for these changes—self service IT, true service orientation, the harnessing of external sources of innovation, and the increased need for integration across multiple service providers. Based on this we identified three new capabilities that IT functions need to acquire to be successful in the era of cloud computing. These are the need to be an "orchestrator of services", for IT to "act as a venture capitalist" and to become the "enterprise app store". We also introduced the IBM Component Business Model as an analytical tool that can help IT management map their analysis of what needs to change down to the next level of organization and process, and considered how ITIL can also help in an analysis of the need for new service management processes. We believe that these changes together represent something we call a "new constitution" for IT.

Higher Education and Cloud Computing: A Match Made in Heaven
Dutch University Shedding Client/Server Past for Cloud-Centric Future

There are few environments where cloud computing makes more sense than in higher education. The combination of thousands of young people who've been raised in the Internet age, all needing access to a variety of information and applications, and all increasingly wanting to do so from anywhere on campus and off, adds up to an ideal setting for capitalizing fully on the cloud's potential.

That's certainly what they're realizing at Windesheim, a 20,000-student university of applied sciences in The Netherlands that has been moving steadily from a client/server IT model toward one that emphasizes the cloud. "We have a goal that every application we use has to be online," says Windesheim's CIO and IT director, Rob Keemink.

The school started out slowly a few years ago, rolling out an Intranet, built on Microsoft Sharepoint, that functions more than anything as a clearing house for request forms. When any of the school's 2,000 staff members need anything, from a new employee to software to classroom supplies, they use the forms to state their need, specify any known costs, and then track the progress of their request.

From there, it was on to a growing array of Web-based services. For example, Blackboard gives teachers and students around-the-clock access to class-related information ranging from assignment details to class cancellation notifications; an application called iExpense enables staff to file expense reports online; and another app, Educator, simplifies the distribution and increases the accuracy of posted grades.

School Encountering Many Opportunities to Benefit From Cloud

The opening of a second campus in the fall of 2010 has given the school a convenient opportunity to further establish a cloud-friendly infrastructure. Keemink hopes to provide students on the new campus with web-based email accounts from Google or Microsoft, either of which offers much more storage than the school can within its current email environment. Doing so will greatly reduce the need for servers to support the new campus' computing requirements. (Web-based email and data residing on Microsoft or Google servers is not an option for

93

staff due to Dutch privacy regulations and the fact that emails and data containing personal data might pass through, or reside on, servers in other countries.)

Cloud computing also is allowing Windesheim to scale back on its existing IT hardware. Keemink says the school's current server room, which is located on the original campus and houses 300 app servers and 40 TB of disk storage, will be consolidated over the next 5 to 10 years as more of the school's computing resources shift to the cloud.

Keemink points out that one of the main drivers pushing the school aggressively toward the cloud is that it no longer makes sense to support today's students with traditional IT architectures. "It's completely normal for them to have their data, their information about school, at every moment, wherever they are," he says.

Cloud's Impact is Reaching Far Beyond Student Population

Teachers are quickly moving that way, too, as they increasingly see the benefits of Web-based access to applications and services. But getting the school's board to understand the new direction was a bit trickier.

Keemink says that when he first tried to explain cloud computing to board members, they had a hard time grasping it. For instance, he had set up a Wiki as a collaborative tool for managing campus planning over the next few years, but board members didn't understand what a Wiki was. He provided them with access, and now they use the Wiki to discuss documents during meetings, rather than bringing hard copies with them. It's helped convince them that cloud computing brings significant value to students, teachers, and the school's IT operation.

In addition to that value, cloud computing has brought great change to Windesheim's IT staff. The required skill set has been shifting to building applications, managing projects and overseeing cloud contracts rather than staffing help desks or watching over servers, networks and storage equipment. "We're seeing another kind of staff that's more highly educated," says Keemink. "It's another kind of work in IT now."

It's not just that: It's a whole new way of running a business. Or, in this case, a school.

6 Enterprise Architecture for Cloud's Sake

6.1 Introduction

The role of enterprise architecture (EA) was already touched upon in the previous chapters. As stated in Chapter 2, the enterprise architecture team is an absolutely essential group to help guide the adoption and governance of all things "cloud." It is an essential part of the broker function discussed in Chapters 4 and 5. It has to make sure that different cloud services will be adopted in a coherent and well-integrated fashion. In this chapter we will further explain the role of enterprise architecture. We will make the point that without EA, cloud computing is expected to have a negative effect on costs and agility. We will also dive into what makes up an EA practice and we will introduce dynamic enterprise architecture as an effective way to manage architecture in an organization. As a good EA practice depends heavily on people, we will discuss some of the dilemma's these people have to deal with such as continuously balancing the short and long term effects of any change. Finally we will discuss some EA-deliverables such as principles, reference models and patterns that can be of great help in making decisions as to what might be candidates for cloud services and what would definitively not be.

6.2 Cloud Computing Requires Coherence and Integration

Cloud computing is more than just infrastructure. It's a way of obtaining anything as a service, whether it's software, data or infrastructure, from different kinds of providers via the Internet. In this context, a service is a reusable component: a piece that supports a business process executed by the business to create value.

Cloud computing is a very attractive model for users. It's quite easy for them to purchase services. The big value of enterprise architecture in this context is that the total landscape of services and solutions of an organization remains or becomes well integrated. Enterprise architecture is the discipline that guides the organization towards a coherent and well-integrated set of services and solutions—not just technology, but also business processes and applications. If you don't pay attention to EA, a couple of years from now your corporate data may be spread across many places, your company may be relying on way too many unreliable partners, the whole conglomerate of internal and external IT may have become impossible to change and the expected benefits of the cloud will have turned into a liability. If you are serious about adopting cloud computing, it requires a long-term vision and strategy: moving into the cloud is not a short-term visit, but a long-term structured journey.

The expected effect of EA on the adoption of cloud computing is shown in the Figures 6.1 and 6.2. Though not scientific, these figures are based on our many years of experience with EA and the adoption of other technologies and models such as SOA. The graphs show an effect that we expect to happen with cloud too: agility and lower cost of ownership *in the long run* do not happen automatically..

Figure 6.1 demonstrates the expected impact on agility of adopting cloud computing in two scenarios: one with EA and one without EA. If cloud computing is adopted without attention to coherence and integration, agility may improve in the very short term, but unfortunately it will deteriorate. Agility deteriorates because of the ever-increasing complexity of the landscape, because of services that are not integrated, and because of the increasing difficulties of switching from one cloud provider to another. On the other hand, if cloud computing is adopted within an EA context, agility improves dramatically over time. The effect will even be bigger if you already have a well-established EA practice.

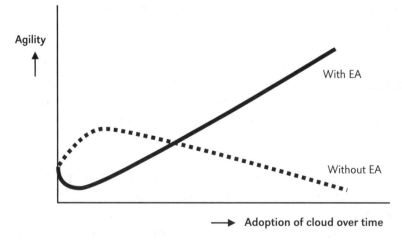

Figure 6.1: Effect of EA on agility when adopting cloud computing

The expected effect on costs (of running IT) is visualized in Figure 6.2. By applying cloud computing, the costs of running IT (operations and maintenance) are likely to decrease dramatically. If users are allowed to buy whatever cloud services they like, without looking out for coherence and integration, the effect can be even bigger in the short term. But after some time, the IT costs will start to rise dramatically, due to the increasing complexity and difficulty of changing services and solutions. If cloud computing is adopted in a structured fashion where the EA team sets the principles and standards for cloud adoption, the cost of running IT will also start to decrease, but in a steady and prolonged fashion.

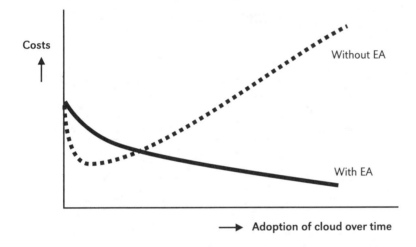

Figure 6.2: Effect of EA on IT costs after adopting cloud computing

It might be clear from the foregoing that EA is geared to the long term by providing principles, standards and patterns for integration and coherence. But what should an effective EA team look like in the cloud era? Self-provisioning users want support, guidance and training rather than policing by a policy department.

6.3 Dynamic Enterprise Architecture

The EA team in the organization should become supportive and proactive, famous for saying "yes" instead of "no" and for accelerating the business and coming up with business ideas.

How to make EA more supportive and pro-active? Figure 6.3 contains a model where EA is positioned as a support process instead of an autonomous process that is not aligned with the rest of the organization. Doing enterprise architecture like the model suggests ensures the integration and coherence of cloud initiatives, on the one hand, while on the other hand it guarantees that architects are involved from the beginning, in the strategic dialogue where they can help the organization take the right steps to the cloud at the right moment. The architects are thus being supportive and proactive instead of hindering and reactive.

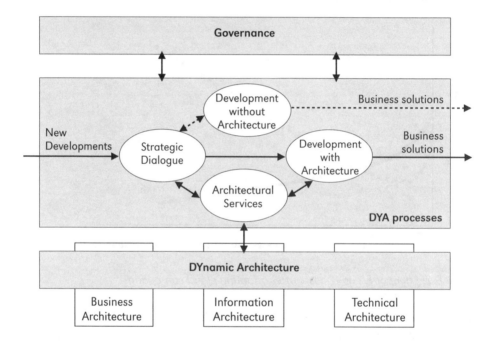

Figure 6.3: DYA model

What is DYnamic Architecture (DYA®)?

DYA is a set of best practices to achieve an effective enterprise architecture (Wagter 2005; Berg and Steenbergen 2006).

At the heart of DYA is the DYA model that consists of four (sub-) processes covering the entire process of change, from strategy formation to realization:

- *Strategic dialogue*—through which the business goals are established and elaborated into concrete project proposals by means of business cases. The business goals are discussed in a dialogue between business and IT.

- *Architectural services*—the processes in which the architecture is formulated and then made available for the strategic dialogue and development with architecture.
- *Development with architecture*—in which the business goals are achieved within the stipulated time frames and in accordance with the anticipated quality and costs—in the DYA process, development with architecture is the standard.
- *Development without architecture*—a deliberate choice in special circumstances, perhaps involving extreme time pressure, to deviate from the architectural framework.

In this model, architectural services (such as the development and maintenance of architecture) clearly constitute a support process. Architecture is not a goal in itself, but a tool for managing the changes formulated in the strategic dialogue and realized in development with(out) architecture. It aligns these changes so they can best serve the business goals of the organization. Because the DYA model clearly identifies the key factors involved in architectural practices, it has been adopted by many organizations.

Using the DYA model as a basis for doing EA in the cloud era tells us:
- Cloud computing is not a goal but a means to achieve a business objective. Cloud computing is a model that can function as an enabler. The advantages and opportunities of cloud computing must be discussed in the strategic dialogue. The role of EA in the strategic dialogue is to improve decision making by creating scenarios for cloud adoption. It's not the enterprise architect who makes the decision but business (and IT) management. Enterprise architects combine knowledge of current business (and IT) structures with business objectives and IT possibilities to guide the organization in the right direction.
- Cloud computing is implemented using the "just in time, just enough" principle, as this is driven by the organizational business objectives. DYA provides a model in which the business objectives drive the cloud implementation and not the other way around.
- Since EA is involved in the change from the beginning, it can create principles, standards and patterns for cloud adoption in an early phase. This allows EA to help projects in an early stage instead of arriving too late and trying to correct missteps, thereby being perceived as hindering the development. The so-called project start architecture (PSA) has turned out to be a great tool in helping projects in an early stage to apply the right EA principles and standards (Luijpers 2009).

- Within this model, EA principles and standards are created only when there is a business objective that needs architecture. This minimizes the risk that EA will produce an ivory tower fortified against the implementation of cloud computing.
- There is the flexibility to embark on a cloud computing project without architecture, but there needs to be proper consideration of the fact that the deployed cloud services will need to be brought within architecture at a later stage. Of course this should not be the default scenario.

Are you prepared for success?

The following six statements can be used to see whether you already have an effective EA practice in place that is capable of helping to adopt cloud computing. These checks are founded on the DYA model. For each statement, indicate whether you agree. Use a scale from 1 ("I don't agree at all") to 5 ("I fully agree"). After scoring all statements, check your total below.

#	Statement	1 to 5
1	Our EA team has a significant impact on our IT investment portfolio	
2	Our EA is described in a concise set of principles, standards and patterns (instead of thousands of pages of blueprints)	
3	Our EA team is recognized by business (and IT) leaders for providing clear guidance from the very outset of change	
4	Our EA team succeeded in reducing complexity significantly	
5	The way we incorporate anything as a service is part of our EA	
6	All our projects comply with EA	
	Your total score	

Table 6.1: Assess the effectiveness of your enterprise architecture practice

• You have **6–14 points**: you may have some short-term success using stand-alone cloud services, but in the long run it is very likely that you will run into integration problems that will prove costly. You are not in the right position to achieve a coherent and integrated set of services. Consider how to build an effective EA practice.

• You have **15–24 points**: you may have some success using cloud services in limited areas, but the long-term risks of running into integration problems are still high. You are on the right track with your EA practice, but there is still room for improvement. Addressing the remaining steps will help you to achieve a coherent and integrated set of services.

• You have **25–30 points**: you are in an excellent position to take full advantage of the opportunities cloud computing provides. You are in the best position to achieve a coherent and integrated set of services. Give your EA practice a leading role in exploring the cloud.

6.4 **People Make the Practice**

Organizations are becoming increasingly complex. They have become more and more connected and are operating in a very volatile world. The number of new options that cloud computing is offering will make it even more complex. The EA practice has to deal with this complexity and find ways to cope with it. This requires the EA practice to be composed of people who have the ability to understand the drivers for this complexity and who can explain to senior management what the options are in for example interacting with customers or designing the operations process. Enterprise architects have to be able to handle tough dilemma's, like balancing the short term effect against the long term effect, the opportunistic versus the structural. Although well-integrated solutions might be everybody's wish, in some circumstances a point solution might be the best choice. In all cases the enterprise architect should be able to explain the consequences and guide the organization to help achieve its objectives in a coherent and integrated way while at the same time coping with its complexity.

Another important role for an EA practice in the cloud era is to scan the market for cloud services. This market research role fits into the broker function of an internal IT department. By playing this role enterprise architects can proactively engage with the business to help them benefit from the opportunities cloud computing offers instead of waiting for initiatives elsewhere in the organization. This will help them to become famous for saying "yes" instead of notorious for saying "no".

Here are the main requirements for an effective enterprise architect:
- Excellent communication skills.
- Highly creative.
- Skills to both analyze and synthesize.
- Ability to separate the "what" from the "how." In other words, has the skills to design services from a function point of view instead of a construction point of view.
- Sound understanding of business drivers, objectives and processes.
- Sound understanding of the latest IT trends and developments.
- Sound understanding of the organization's IT landscape.
- Ability to create a vision.
- Ability to connect a vision with measurable business benefits and costs.
- Ability to think outside-in instead of inside-out.
- Leadership.
- Proactive instead of reactive attitude.

It will be nearly impossible to find all of these in one person. But in a team, these skills and abilities can and must be present.

6.5 Principles First

Architecture principles are a widely accepted starting point for describing enterprise architecture. Principles are general rules and guidelines, intended to be enduring and seldom amended, that inform and support the way in which an organization sets about fulfilling its mission. They define the underlying general rules and guidelines for the use and deployment of all IT resources and assets across the enterprise. They reflect a level of consensus among the various elements of the enterprise, and form the basis for making future (IT) decisions (The Open Group 2009). Similarly, architecture principles provide an excellent starting point in the case of cloud computing. They can be used to decide on and communicate the future place of cloud services in the organization. Principles can also be used to point out the strategic advantages to adopting cloud computing.

Examples of architecture principles relevant to the cloud	
Name:	**Cloud First**
Statement:	If sourcing decisions will be made about non critical services, cloud computing is the first option to consider
Rationale:	• Cost reduction • Agility
Implications:	• A list of software and infrastructure services must be available that clarifies which are critical and which are not critical • Criteria exist about when to deviate from cloud computing
Name:	**Design anything as a service**
Statement:	Our business and IT is designed in terms of services
Rationale:	• Agility • Flexibility
Implications:	• Templates are available for how to design a service • All relevant sectors like business development, EA and IT program management know how to design services • A repository is available with all services and their status • A service will only be designed if it has a clear owner

Examples of architecture principles relevant to the cloud (cont.)

Name:	Commoditize business services unless
Statement:	IT will commoditize business services to a large extent unless the business has a business case not to do so
Rationale:	• Cost reduction • Increase reuse • Agility
Implications:	• A list of business services is available that distinguishes between the services that will be commoditized and those that will be maintained. A way to make that distinction is to list the 100 business services the IT department delivers, ranking them in priority from those that create most revenue or business differentiation. Then, draw a line at #25. Everything below that line will be commoditized, while everything above that line will be maintained. • A process is in place to allow the business to come up with a business case to prevent IT from commoditizing a particular service.

6.6   Reference Models Provide a Map for Cloud Adoption

Principles, standards and patterns are at the heart of enterprise architecture and important EA artefacts to guide cloud adoption. Reference models can also add value in cloud adoption. These models can be used to decide which components could be deployed in the cloud and which could not. A reference model is not a design to strive for but a model for basing decisions upon. It functions as a map for cloud adoption. In the case of cloud computing, it is important to create a reference model that is composed in a service-oriented way. That makes it easier to discover available services somewhere in the cloud that match the required services. A reference model is broad in scope and encompasses more than the cloud: it can be used as a roadmap for service adoption irrespective of the source of these services.

The risk of creating reference models is that enterprise architects can get lost in their models. Be careful to create these models only when there is clear objective. Providing guidance for cloud adoption is such a reason.

Below we will introduce two different approaches that you can use to create reference models. One is based on capability modeling and the other on essential modeling. You will see that there are differences, but also that the approaches can be complementary.

Capability modeling as starting point

In this section three different reference models will be discussed:

1. Business reference model
2. Application reference model
3. Application area reference model

Business reference model

This model is the foundation and starting point for architecture reference modeling. The most valuable type of model for cloud and SOA is the capability model (Berg *et al.* 2007). Figure 6.4 shows the basic structure of such a model.

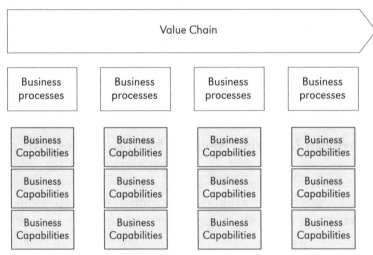

Figure 6.4: Business reference model

The value chain perspective is important for putting the business processes into a context. The next step is to divide the value chain into relevant business processes or domains. Next, divide those business processes into capabilities. Capabilities say on a high level *what* a business does.

The model is not a detailed distinct process model, but a model with components that can be used to build real business process scenarios. The idea of capability modeling is to provide a structure that promotes future business agility. If IT solutions are built on detailed processes they will (sooner or later) hinder strategic business changes. If they are built on capabilities, they will support and enable changes.

The business reference model should be used in all business development discussions. This helps to steer towards the cloud and fuels a dialogue based on SOA. It also creates a common language and view of the future business. When designing this model it is necessary to involve business stakeholders. This in itself is an opportunity for the architects to strengthen the relationship and build trust within the business.

The most comprehensive and proven support for business capability modelling is the Component Business Model (CBM) from IBM. CBM also consists of ready-made industry models open for reuse.

Application reference model

The first very tangible value from a cloud perspective comes when the application reference model is defined. This reference model consists of application areas, which are a set of large application components. It is useful for finding software services in the cloud that match these components. Figure 6.5 contains a simple example that shows the modeling principle.

Once the business reference model is established, the task is to sort the capabilities into application areas. It may seem easy, but don't take it too casually. This is a very important foundation for all forthcoming cloud architectural work. If the division is wrong, you may end up in a situation where there are no services available in the cloud that match with the defined application areas, or even no standard products available at all. The idea is that the areas, as far as possible without destroying the business model, shall match services and applications available on the market, while fulfilling the strategic IT goals.

In the example above, two typical application areas are derived from the business model: Product Lifecycle Management (PLM) and Customer Relationship Management (CRM). The connection with the business model is important because it clarifies once and for all which business functions are supported by which application areas. Another interesting aspect when working with business and application reference models is that common service areas may come to surface. In the example above, sourcing is a potential common service. Common means that it may be used in more than one business process. Sourcing is a capability under product management in the figure above, but it will also be a capability in new product supply, after market management and plant maintenance processes. As a common service, sourcing is a possible cloud service.

Application area reference model

The application reference model consists of application areas, which are further detailed in application area reference models. The important thing about these models is that they clearly show the information and services perspectives. Figure 6.6 is an example of what to aim for.

105

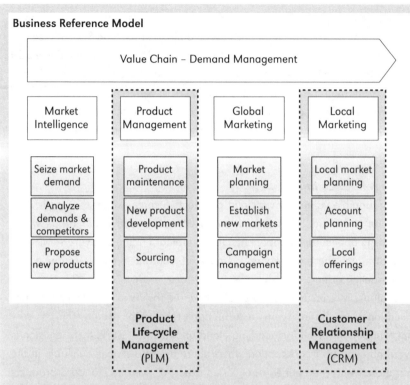

Figure 6.5: Example of an application reference model

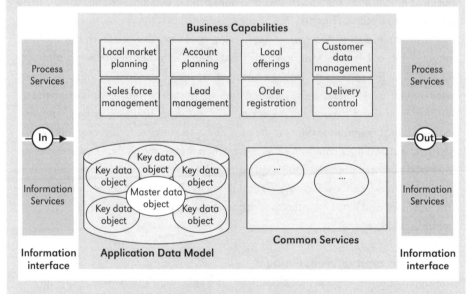

Figure 6.6: Application area reference model for CRM

Figure 6.6 demonstrates:

- What business capabilities the application area shall support, or in other words, what basic functionality it shall contain.
- What key data the application needs to be able to handle autonomously (application data model). An application area can be the master of certain data objects.
- The information interface describes the needed information flows *in* and *out* from the application area. Information flows are of two main types: information flows connected to more or less automated business processes (process services) and information services that are related to real-time demand-response behavior.
- Common services are services that are shared by many application areas. In the CRM example above, a common service from Dun & Bradstreet (DnB) for cleaning customer data is a typical example.

Application area reference models of the style described above are very useful in cloud assessments. When analyzing the use of an application as a service, the functional and information context is sufficiently clear. The requirements for integration can easily be derived. The information interfaces and common services may also be interesting to analyze from a cloud perspective. To buy *one* enterprise service from DnB instead of many locally agreed services is very likely a business case. One global health care provider used a cloud-provided information service for transformation to and from the global HL7 standard format. That's another tangible example of using cloud for a small service in the daily operations.

Application area reference models are also very valuable tools when working with standardization and consolidation efforts around the application map within an enterprise. The models are the structure to aim for, and the information interfaces are the first level to achieve in the standardization roadmap. If an enterprise has many different systems supporting one application area, the first step is to harmonize the information interfaces. The second step is to replace the applications. This is a simple strategy to achieve as seamless a transformation as possible. When the interfaces are standardized, it naturally opens up the question about the application area as a cloud service.

The next approach is based on modeling the essential processes of an organization.

Essential modeling as starting point

The term "cloud services" implies service orientation. Service orientation requires thinking in services, not just in shaping IT, but fundamentally and more importantly, in shaping the business. This shaping should be done in such a way that requisite supporting services are identified and defined in the resulting (business) model. In these reference models it is still undecided whether a particular service will be obtained from the cloud or in some other way.

Thinking in services also requires overview and insight to be able to define a consistent and coherent set of services, at an appropriate level of granularity: at the business level. The total set of services required in a specific business context must be clearly identified and for each identified service it should be clear how, why and when it is used, from a business perspective.

Business processes are key in shaping the business of an organization. However, the commonly used process models are based on flowcharts with lots of operational details. These models are not very well suited for shaping the organization. Instead we prefer to view the processes at the essential level as a basis for service orientation and for many other purposes such as controlling and steering an organization or doing impact analyses before starting projects.

The notion of *essential processes* and its contribution to using cloud services in an effective way is explained below using a simple example. Essential processes do not replace existing (operational) processes, but represent a view of these processes based on what is essential for doing business. Essential processes also provide structure and coherence across all relevant processes, which is too often absent, and are by nature a "coat rack" for the more detailed processes (the coats). Essential processes focus on the use of business processes as a steering aid for management.

Imagine a simple Online Book Store. The essential model for this book store starts with its rationale for existence: there are customers who want to buy books over the Internet.

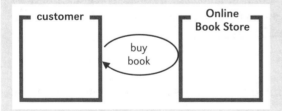

Figure 6.7: Essential model

In order to get the book to the customer, the Online Book Store needs to do business with other "parties" (business domains). In this case the business domains are the book distributor (where the books are in stock) and the delivering party (which could be part of the Online Book Store or some third party). Also, the customer needs to pay before the book will be delivered (Figure 6.8).

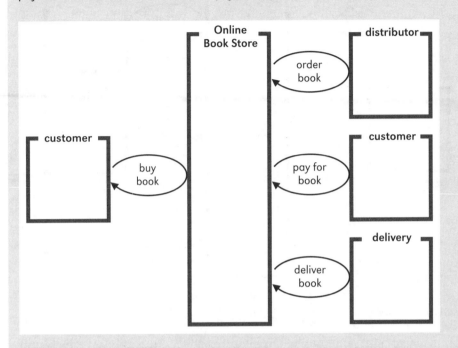

Figure 6.8: Essential model including business domains

The model basically shows the accountable business domains involved in handling the customer request and the way these domains work together.

Doing business is indicated by the transaction symbol: the customer needs something, the supplier provides it (or not) and the customer accepts the result (or not).

In addition to being connected through transactions, parties can also be connected by the exchange of information. When looking into the "essentials" of a transaction (such as buying books) information requirements pop up (for example, the need to register customer information). This in turn identifies the need for an information object (customer), which will also be used by the delivering party to obtain the delivery address (Figure 6.9).

These elements (business domains, business transactions and business information objects) to a large extent shape the *essential* business processes. There is more to the concept of essential processes, but for the purpose of this example the above is sufficient to illustrate its use in relation to cloud services:

1. Each transaction by nature is a business service: one party needs something and the other provides it (and the transaction defines how business is done).

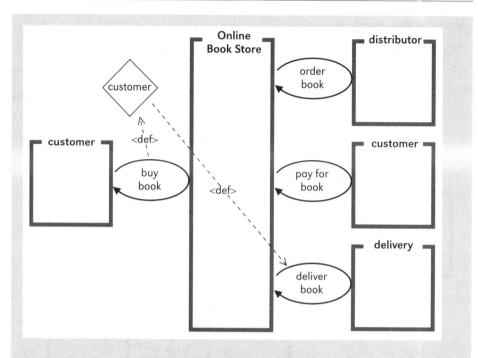

Figure 6.9: Essential model including information objects

2. Each link (dotted arrow) to an information object also indicates a business (information) service: the nature of the service (*e.g.* register name, address and bank account number of a customer) is defined in the arrow.

The set of services appearing in all essential process models of the enterprise is a perfect starting point for acquiring these services, whether via the cloud or otherwise (Noorman 2006).

As can be seen above different approaches can be followed to create reference models. Essential modeling might be the right approach when working from the outside. Capability modeling works better if the perspective is from the inside. When analyzing opportunities for the cloud, both approaches can be used next to another: the outside-in approach to derive the right set of (future) services, the inside-out approach to discover which current systems and services to migrate to the cloud.

6.7   **Focus on Function Instead of Construction**

On the journey to obtain services from the cloud, it is very important to know what functionality is required by those services, with what quality and how these services fit in an organization's landscape as a whole. However, it is often seen that foremost and most attention is paid to the (technical) construction of services. This is encouraged by many cloud providers, who have put their proposition in technical terms, combined with service-level characteristics. Of course, at a certain point in time during the integration of cloud services, the way the services are technically constructed becomes important. At least in order to safeguard reliability, consistency, interoperability and user friendliness, to name a few aspects.

But before focusing on the "how" of cloud and the many (different) propositions that are offered from the many corners of the cloud, a concise architectural overview of the organization's landscape is indispensable as a compass on the cloud journey. It facilitates the identification and classification of functional components and patterns that deliver business services and, as such, are present in the IT landscape. On an architectural level, functions and patterns are technologically "agnostic" and therefore very stable. They are independent of the current and even future way of implementation. This means that these functions and patterns stay the same in a "cloud world." Of course, obtaining a service from the cloud might lead to a more important role for integration functions (like identity and permission validation). But essentially, these functions and patterns stay the same. This is especially valid for infrastructure or technical architecture, but is not limited to these architecture domains. This way of working is also recommended in the areas of business and information architecture in order to determine what might be deployed in the cloud and what should definitely not be. This was illustrated in the previous chapter.

The more things change, the more they stay the same

What is a pattern?
A pattern is a typical and repeatable way a solution is commonly provided or a problem fixed. Patterns exist at several levels of abstraction, from architecture to engineering and construction. At the architectural level, sheer functionality is targeted, defined in such a way that it is technologically agnostic. A pattern consists of a combination of functions that together provide a solution. In fact, the whole IT landscape could be

regarded as a pattern. For practical reasons, this pattern is divided into sub-patterns that are interrelated. Each sub-pattern describes a part of the landscape that offers some (recognizable) sort of solution. An example of an infrastructure architecture (sub-)pattern is given next:

Application hosting pattern type

Definition
The pattern type application hosting describes the architectural layout of solutions that accommodate applications by providing a runtime environment and a set of additional facilities that support the execution and integration of applications in the IT landscape.

Graphical overview

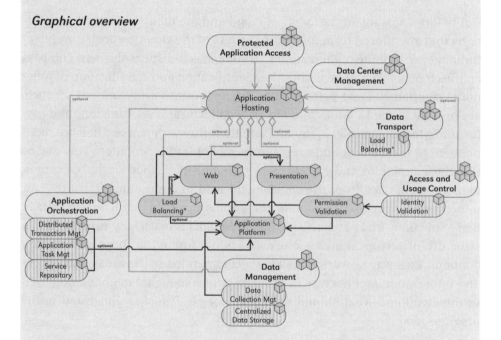

Figure 6.10: Pattern type application hosting—ArchiMate visualization

Composition
This pattern type is made up of the primary building block types listed in Table 6.2.

Building Block Type	Purpose	Character
Application Platform	Provides a runtime environment for application code, by means of system resources and a library of standard routines.	Mandatory
Permission Validation	Checks user permissions regarding access and usage of application parts and/or data.	Optional
Presentation	Delivers output of applications towards application clients (screen handling), and handles input from those clients (most commonly by keyboard and mouse).	Optional
Web	Delivers handling of application input and output in the form of webpages.	Optional
Load Balancing	Distributes client connections between separate instances of the same application. This kind of functionality can be applied during data transport or be carried out by these application instances themselves.	Optional

Table 6.2: Building block types for pattern application hosting

The adjacent pattern types provide facilities that realize the integration of application hosting within the IT landscape listed in Table 6.3.

Adjacent Pattern Type	Building Block Types	Purpose
Data Management	Data Collection Management	Organization and logical deposition of application data.
	Centralized Data Storage	Physical storage of application data on a centralized facility. When used by application hosting, in many cases the physical storage is not in use by the application itself, but by the data collection management facility.
Data Transport	Network Access	Access to data transport resources to all systems/platforms that are involved in providing facilities of the pattern type application hosting.
	Load Balancing	Distributes client connections between separate instances of the same application. This kind of functionality can be applied during data transport or be carried out by these application instances themselves.

Adjacent Pattern Type	Building Block Types	Purpose
Access and Usage Control (optional)	Identity Validation	Checks if provided identity claims (for example, logon names that identify a certain user, together with passwords or other types of credentials) can be validated against stored credentials.
Application Orchestration (optional)	Distributed Transaction Management	Direction of data processing that is being carried out by more than one application (instance).
	Application Task Management	Directs at what time and/or in what order an application should process tasks.
	Service Repository	Automated overview of, and pointers towards, (external) application routines.

Table 6.3: Adjacent pattern types for pattern application hosting

All patterns at the architectural level of abstraction are formed by a combination of typical, technology agnostic functions. A complete collection of generic definitions of infrastructure functions and patterns of this type can be found at Sogeti's DYA Infrastructure Repository (see Sogeti in the Reference section of this book).

Based on a functional overview of an organization's landscape, the cloud journey can be planned responsibly. It is possible to determine which functions, in which usage context, are feasible candidates to obtain from the cloud. Clearly, it will be easier to find a very common application hosting service than a very specific scientific computing solution. And although it makes sense to give standard office workers access to office automation solutions by means of a web server, it might not be a good idea to try to provide a check-in kiosk at an airport by means of cloud services. So, to be sure that you get the right services from the cloud, you should first examine what functionality is needed, with what desired quality, and then start looking for feasible solutions. What used to be good practice on occasion needs to become the norm as more and more possible solutions are deliverable from the cloud. And by discussing functionality over technology every stakeholder can play a part in the discourse.

6.8 **Conclusion**

An enterprise architecture practice is invaluable in successfully adopting a service-oriented approach and therefore also in adopting cloud computing. When cloud computing is adopted without EA the risk is high that costs will increase over time and that agility will deteriorate rather than improve. Cloud computing, as any IT element, requires integration and coherency. This is the main task for EA and has everything to do with helping the organization cope with its complexity. Cloud computing also offers an opportunity for EA's. When they take on the market research role for cloud services, they can proactively help the organization to quickly adopt the most business valuable cloud services.

In order to be successful EA must be implemented in a dynamic fashion, populated with the right set of skills, designed with a concise set of principles and reference models, and focused on the function of services instead of the construction. Capability modeling and essential modeling are powerful ways to discover the right set of services as a starting point to research the market for providers of these services. Design patterns are very useful in searching the right cloud services because they focus on the function of IT instead of the construction.

If done right, enterprise architecture will help to overcome cloud barriers like integration. However, there are other cloud barriers to overcome. These will be discussed in the next chapter.

ING Looks to Slash Fixed IT Costs by Adopting Hybrid Cloud Model
IT Strategy Evolves to Reap Benefits of Cloud Computing

Sometimes, in order to find the most obvious answer to a problem, one must first walk down several paths. Just ask Tony Kerrison.

Last year, the head of infrastructure services of Dutch financial services giant ING Group got approval to pursue an aggressive infrastructure refresh that would see the company consolidate 16 data centers into just two, with state-of-the-art power and cooling systems. ING would build the data centers itself, and bring them online in 2012.

A funny thing happened on the way to those new data centers, though: As Kerrison and his team embarked on an aggressive virtualization and application rationalization program, they decided it made sense to establish a private cloud environment. From there, it wasn't long before the discussion shifted to which of ING's applications could actually live in a cloud environment.

And just like that, building data centers didn't sound so good.

"When you're sitting there looking at an investment like that, you find yourself wondering, should ING be building two data centers in 2011?" says Kerrison. "We'd be looking at two empty rooms in a few years time."

Instead, ING plans to be the anchor tenant for two data centers that will be built by a third-party infrastructure provider. One-third of those facilities will serve as ING's private cloud, and the other two-thirds will be a semi-private cloud in which infrastructure could be shared among multiple companies, but with their applications and data residing on separate servers. ING's mission-critical applications will be placed in the private cloud environment, while apps that have more spiky computing needs could reside in the semi-private cloud, where capacity can be dialed up and down as business conditions warrant.

IT Focus Shifting From Infrastructure to Workload Management

Kerrison has a clear goal in transitioning ING from a company that manages its own IT infrastructure to one that is instead focused on managing workloads in a hybrid environment: He wants to convert as much of the company's fixed IT costs and assets into variable as he possibly can. That way, as cloud services are adopted throughout the company, he'll minimize the financial drain by giving IT maximum cost flexibility.

"Our businesses will start to see how they can go to cloud providers and get lower cost, better services than we can provide internally," says Kerrison. "What will happen if we don't pay attention is that we will sit on a fixed cost base, and the variable cost base will move outside the company. The result will be more IT costs."

Kerrison estimates that ING is saving "many millions" of Euros by avoiding the costs of building its own data centers. Some of those savings are being used to ensure that ING's IT employees are ready for the cloud, which will change the skills required of them. Specifically, ING is launching an effort to provide foundation-level training on virtualization and cloud technologies for all IT employees, with more detailed training being provided for those who'll work most closely with the technologies.

Parallel to this, the company has forged a partnership with some of the biggest IT vendors—including IBM, Microsoft, Cisco, Google and HP—to create a certification program for working with virtualization and cloud technologies. Kerrison believes the combination of training and certification not only will ensure that his staff is able to extract the maximum value from the cloud; he'll also ensure his employees are as employable as possible for their future careers.

Company Being Careful Not to Bite Off More than It Can Chew

ING's emerging cloud strategy represents a dramatic change for a company that, only a year ago, had what Kerrison described as a "less mature" attitude toward the cloud. Now, he foresees ING developing an increasing focus on delivering convenient services to its customers via the cloud.

"The time to market is going to be incredible," says Kerrison. "We'll have the ability to serve the client faster and react to market conditions better than we've ever done before."

That said, Kerrison remains realistic. He says ING's most critical in-house applications won't be placed into the cloud any time in the next few years. Rather, the company will focus initially on its infrastructure-as-a-service plans, as well as placing utility applications into the cloud, before it starts considering turning its banking products into cloud-based services.

ING will take advantage of that gradual transition by making itself comfortable with the cloud. It is clear that regulatory requirements, privacy and security will remain key factors in the adoption to cloud services. As these develop and mature, companies will be able to enjoy the full benefits of cloud computing.

"You're going to get to the point that you can arbitrage cloud providers based on their prices and the services, and very easily move your workload around," says Kerrison.

It sounds suspiciously like the IT-as-utility model IT executives have long been waiting for.

7 Overcoming the Barriers

7.1 Introduction

Saying "it can never be secure" seems to be the weapon of choice with which critics try to shoot down any talk of adopting cloud computing. When they are pushed a bit more, a score of other objections are brought to the table that would scare even the bravest of CIO's. At the same time, there are the examples of banks, medical research companies, government agencies, hospitals, schools, and so forth, all of whom found a way around these objections and adopted cloud computing in some shape or form. The reality of it is, of course, that what for one man can be a barrier, something that prevents adoption, someone else might see as simply one of the steps to take, or one of the challenges to overcome. In the end, it should just be a matter of checking to see if the benefits outweigh the costs and the risk in any specific situation.

7.2 Weighing the Issues

With a broad topic such as cloud computing, it may feel logical to examine it as a pattern to apply to everything we do or even to the entire industry. When we look at it this way, we may discard cloud because we feel it doesn't fit one or some of our activities. Only later do we realize that it may be useful and valuable in some areas and not in others: cloud computing will become part of the bag of tricks of any organization. In a sense, there is a parallel with the original introduction of the Internet and email. Many of the same risks and objections were raised then: unsecure, unreliable and sometimes an unclear ROI. Over time, organizations have figured out where they can and cannot use these technologies.

Whether you use cloud for most of your IT, for some of it, or if you stay away from cloud as much as possible, will depend on how big the risks are, and to what extent you can counter or overcome them. Don't adopt cloud for simplistic reasons, but also don't discard it before a good analysis.

In the rest of this chapter, we'll discuss the common objections and how you could overcome them. The intent here is not to sell the cloud or trivialize the risks, but to provide a balanced way to think about the risks and costs that are part of the complete picture.

These are often mentioned as potential barriers to cloud computing:
- "Cloud can never be secure"
- "Our regulations prohibit the cloud"
- "Cloud is too expensive"
- "Cloud has no business value"
- "It's easy to get in, impossible to get out"
- "Integration is impossible"
- "Migration to the cloud is too hard"
- "Too difficult to keep control"
- "Performance and stability are insufficient"
- "The reputation risk is too large"
- "The cloud providers are not guaranteed future-proof"
- "Lack of internal cloud expertise"
- "The large systemic risks are too large for society"

7.3   Cloud Can Never Be Secure

The issue: As soon as data flows elsewhere it can be stolen, changed or viewed. Credit card information, health records, personal records or intellectual property may be stolen. Clients may sue, or marketing scandals could cost millions.

How you could address it: For one, not all cloud solutions are equally secure or insecure. A security analysis of the chosen solution is warranted. To improve security, many technical patterns are available and widely tested that guarantee security of communication channels, encryption of data while in storage, *etc*. The first, simple, approach is to create a good secure system that is designed for the infrastructure that it runs on. And while the traditional view is that to keep things safe, they need to stay inside your own walls, the reality is that 50% or more (depending on the study) of security breaches are by internal agents (RisknCompliance 2010). Perhaps the cloud could actually help make IT more secure?

Or as Mike Bradshaw, director of Google Federal, put it in a thought-provoking way in a July 1, 2010 article in *Computerworld* (Gross 2010): *"Despite the concerns, cloud computing will improve security. Cloud computing vendors store data on multiple servers in multiple locations, making it difficult for cyber criminals to target one location. The redundancy also means agencies are protected against disasters."* He added: *"The cloud enhances security by enabling data to be stored centrally with continuous and automated network analysis and protection. When vulnerabilities are detected they can be managed more rapidly and uniformly. Cloud security is able to respond to attacks more rapidly by reducing the time it takes to install patches on thousands of individual desktops or hundreds of uniquely configured on-premise servers."*

Part of this security risk is real, part is perception. Hiring some security experts or even ethical hackers can pinpoint the real problems and fortify your defenses while you move to the cloud.

Key takeaway: This is by far the most often mentioned objection to cloud computing, yet it is not very specific. The reality is much more nuanced. Some real risks exist, and with more cloud adoption, the interest in hacking the cloud may grow. So build or hire the expertise, address the issues early and choose your solutions wisely.

7.4 Our Regulations Prohibit the Cloud

The issue: Some organizations are under a lot of regulation regarding privacy, data-security or auditing. Especially in Europe, the regulations with regard to privacy are very strict, and many governments do not allow certain data to flow across the border (Longbottom 2008). In some cases, regulation is simply unclear: when using services from elsewhere, which rules apply?

How you could address it: Working closely with the legal and auditing teams is important. Very often the attitude of these people will make the difference: are they looking for solutions or looking for reasons to say no. There is not one single outcome: some data may very well live in the cloud, other data needs to remain on premise. Much of the same analyses that were done around traditional outsourcing can be applied here. Cloud providers are working hard to conform to industry regulation (for example, HIPAA for healthcare (AWS 2009)) and become transparent enough to withstand auditing. In

Europe, global cloud providers are building local data centers to comply with local privacy regulation.

Key takeaway: Choose the right team and involve them from the start. Examine the options and find where it does (and does not) create insurmountable problems.

7.5   Cloud Is Too Expensive

The issue: The current solution could be cheaper than a cloud alternative. A package based solution costs less in licenses then the per-user license in the cloud. Or perhaps the economics of "unlikely scenarios" (merger or sudden growth of the company) is not in favor of the cloud.

How you could address it: First, make sure you do a fair analysis: both on the cost side and on the benefits side. When calculating internal cost, take into account things that are often forgotten: housing, recruitment cost, electricity, backups, support desk, *etc*. For the external cost, take into account things like the usage cost, network cost, and also the risks you can calculate. Then look into potential business benefits (growth, new products, *etc*.). A useful tool is to create different possible scenarios and estimate the likelihood of each of them occurring. Make sure that all these calculations and estimates are projected over a long period of time and assume that business will change: the benefit of cloud may only become visible when adding up the many projects you've executed to simply apply patches, upgrade versions and incorporate new legislation.

Key takeaway: Often a quick evaluation is misleading. Only if you make a true cost analyses can you start to determine if the investment will be worth it in business terms.

7.6   Cloud Has No Business Value

The issue: Business sponsors see cloud as an IT project that has little to do with them. There is no clear business case or even business rationale.

How you could address it: When this issue pops up, it's most likely a situation where IT has positioned cloud as a mere infrastructural project and the whole cloud endeavor has started as just an IT exercise. Look for business needs and consider highlighting examples such as conference calling, video hosting, messaging and collaboration that will help put cloud more in a business perspective. Chapter 3 of this book, the chapter on business technology, will help. Inspire the business by showing examples of cloud services that are available and relevant to your organization.

Key takeaway: Talking about the cloud as a means to change the organization itself has more chance of success then talking about it as an infrastructure project.

7.7 It's Easy to Get in, Impossible to Get out

The issue: The provisioning is seductively easy, but moving away from the cloud may be impossible once people have gotten used to the cloud option. Data could be locked into the one provider. Services may not be available elsewhere. Migrating out could be difficult and expensive.

How you could address it: Most platforms are very open in allowing you to retrieve all your data. When it comes to preventing lock-in, standards and open API's are important. For your part, an IT and architecture process will guard against accidental lock-in. In general, the more proprietary a cloud service or platform is, the harder it will be to move away from it. Vendors may try to create some lock-in, perhaps similar to the application-server and web-server market. And, also as in the application server market, the special features that cause the potential lock-in can be the ones that are most attractive. In that case, balancing value against giving up some freedom is what should be part of the business case. By using as many standards as possible, you retain most of your freedom. Like migrating something to the cloud, migrating between clouds or from cloud to "on premise" could come at a cost. That cost could be estimated early on and simply included in the calculations as a worst-case scenario.

Key takeaway: Most platforms are open and provide some exit-scenario. Taking the moving-out options into account at the start, as you do when buying traditional packages, will enable the creation of a pragmatic approach.

7.8 Integration Is Impossible

The issue: When using multiple cloud and on-premise solutions, they may not work together seamlessly. It could be hard for data to flow from one cloud to another.

How you could address it: Luckily, this has been recognized as a new market, where both new and old players are offering their services. Middleware players eagerly attach to cloud services. There are even some cloud services that are starting to collaborate intensively among themselves to make connectivity and integration easier: for example, moving data from Salesforce to a direct mailing service, and vice versa. A possible scenario is that several big groups of cloud providers will emerge where in each group all parties work seamlessly together. Standards play a role here too, enabling broad integration. The lowest common denominator may be XML, which enables you to create custom integrations between any two things.

Finally, if you have a mature service-oriented architecture inside your organization, some of the internal-external integrations will become a lot easier and make the incorporation of external services very quick.

Key takeaway: Technology is helpful, and a lot is possible already, but sometimes at a very low, technical level instead of a user-friendly, business level. Your SOA helps.

7.9 Migration to the Cloud Is Too Hard

The issue: Porting existing application to the cloud can only be done after significant rewrite of the application: multi-tenancy, state-less interaction, different platform and storage, *etc*. You'd need to first extract the application from its current environment and then recreate the integration points.

How you could address it: The real question is whether the application itself or only the data must be migrated. In the case of commodity software, replacing is better than transforming. If there really is a need to move an application into the cloud, there are many ways in which it can be done: running virtual machines, building a web-interface or porting to a cloud platform. If data needs to migrated, often some data will stay on premise, depending on the risk and business value.

Key takeaway: If migration is truly warranted, it can surely be done. It becomes a matter of costs and benefits. Especially when migrating among well-known platforms, the issues are clear, and migration should not be difficult. Using off-shore resources and automation would keep the cost down.

7.10 Too Difficult to Keep Control

The issue: Giving away freedom makes it hard to keep overall complexity under control. IT groups end up purchasing services, business users provision their own solutions, and so forth. Redundancy and cost explosion are real risks. The risk is often not truly acknowledged by business users who just want quick solutions.

How you could address it: A facilitative enterprise architecture approach would provide guidelines on how to use cloud and ensure an active role for the IT department in brokering services. Business and IT governance processes should include strong controls that focus on continuously reducing complexity.

Key takeaway: This is the most significant long-term risk when it comes to cost control and efficiency of IT. Many parts of this book aim at addressing this issue specifically.

7.11 Performance and Stability are Insufficient

The issue: The quality of a service may be less than was desired. Connecting to a service over the Internet brings with it the issues of latency (the time it takes for a message to get to and from the service) and transmission speed (the amount of data that can be sent per second). Especially when trying to send large datasets, these may be serious issues. Some services have experienced outages. The exact quality of a service can be unpredictable because of network issues and variable loads from other users at the same time.

How you could address it: If your provider does not deliver the service needed, there is little you can do, apart from asking them to improve their SLA. When it's the quality of the network, sometimes solutions can be found in technology: dedicated lines, distributed architecture, *etc*. When it comes to outages, a striking blog post put this issue somewhat in perspective: "(…) *out-*

ages happen and they are not unique to the Cloud. Natural and human-caused disasters occur. Hurricanes and cable cuts can affect all sorts of infrastructure. As with a traditional datacenter, in-house or outsourced, traditional or in the Cloud, a disaster failover and redundancy strategy should be part of an IT department's general strategy for success or just survival" (Sheehan 2009). When establishing the service quality, you should check more than the technology alone: what's the support organization, what procedures are in place, what are the dependencies at the cloud provider's end.

Key takeaway: Establishing realistic performance expectations, identifying what you really need, and checking the service quality are important elements in the decision process. Good testing of the entire chain would be essential for any service that you deem business critical.

7.12 The Reputation Risk Is Too Large

The issue: For the cloud service provider, an issue with service availability or quality is just a small issue, while for the cloud buyer and end-user the impact can be much larger. This imbalance may result in large differences in priorities. For example, a cloud contract that states "if the service is not available, you will get your subscription money back" does not address the massive loss of revenue that may be the result of a service failure.

How you could address it: Cloud contracts may be fairly fixed, especially when it comes to complete commodity services (platform or storage). Still, a solution to the issue would be to negotiate more organization-specific contracts where the measures of success are part of the payment structure and clear penalties are agreed upon in case of failure to deliver. In cases where that would not be possible, choosing the right workloads for cloud components will be important.

Key takeaway: If you can establish a shared interest, this risk will drop dramatically. If the risk is still too large, choosing a different (sub-) set of workloads would be preferred.

7.13 The Cloud Providers Are Not Guaranteed Future-Proof

The issue: Putting important data, systems or processes in the hands of a third party makes you dependent on the business success of that third party. What happens if they go bankrupt? Will you get your data back? Or what happens if they merge with your largest competitor—would they share your secrets? Or if you're truly dependent on any cloud provider, they could increase their prices over time or change the service they are delivering.

How you could address it: Depending on the size of your organization, you may have different solutions available. For example, where large companies would be taken seriously automatically, smaller organizations may have to gather in a user group to establish buying power. That way they can influence the provider when it comes to features, quality of service and price. In general, choosing more established vendors will somewhat reduce the risk of bankruptcy and radical pricing changes. The least you should do is to ensure that there are easy ways to export and backup your data so you can retrieve it whenever needed. As for pricing stability, this is the flipside of flexible pricing or pay-per-use. If only a fixed budget is available, a contract should be sought that covers the services at this fixed price: trading price flexibility for price certainty.

Key takeaway: This is especially an issue for smaller cloud service providers. Pay special attention to the service level agreement. If you don't consider these risks beforehand, they could turn out to be serious issues afterwards.

7.14 Lack of Internal Cloud Expertise

The issue: A new model requiring new skills always means an initial shortage of those skills. Sometimes, for example, the real security risk is not that the technology doesn't allow a secure solution but that the people implementing the technology are not aware or not skilled enough to apply it. Finding or creating fully rounded cloud experts takes time.

How you could address it: Some simple solutions exist: training, experimentation and connecting to others who already have some experience. Perhaps people with traditional mainframe experience could even help. Strong focus on cloud skills can be achieved by creating a center of excellence or cloud team that initiates the shift. Investing in pro-active scouting of cloud services will build awareness of what's available and it will help you see what is really available today that is relevant for you.

Key takeaway: The issue is more a step in the journey to cloud adoption than a real barrier that stands in the way.

7.15 The Systemic Risks Are Too Large for Society

The issue: When systems are connected and shared, they become a system of systems. They start to influence each other in sometimes unpredictable ways. If at the same time multiple companies in the same industry are using these systems, the entire industry or even the global economy could be at risk. For example, if every bank were to host one crucial system on Amazon's cloud, a failure of that cloud would bring the country's financial system to a standstill. Or when many companies use the same service and all of them have peak loads at the same time because of an industry event, the overall capacity may simply not be sufficient to serve all of them.

How you could address it: At the highest level, there are thoughts about some sort of Internet regulator entity, which could keep track of these systemic risks and try to reduce them by creating rules and policies. As banking and healthcare have regulators to ensure the stability and safety of their sectors, so would an Internet regulator play a role. At the organizational level, probably not much risk exists today: not enough organizations use cloud for critical processes, and the cloud usage is not yet very connected or integrated. If you had to address it, it would be through diversification (deliberately choosing multiple vendors) and resilience (creating flexible and unbreakable services and calamity solutions for backup and recovery). You could ask the cloud vendor how much "spare" capacity they have to serve high peak loads, in the way you might ask a bank how much money they have to cover all the accounts.

Key takeaway: This is not a barrier that is very real at the moment, but theoretically it could become much larger as cloud adoption grows. Ultimately it will be for the cloud providers to address this issue and make it part of their service offering.

7.16 Culture or Overall Reluctance to Change

The issue: Changing from *internal* to *external* implies a shift in activities and functions. Reducing the number of server administrators would leave them looking for extensive retraining or new jobs. The people who have to enable the change will be reluctant to initiate it for fear of losing their own position. This goes for the developers and administrators, up to the CIO: if the role of IT is changing, what will be my role? Even more basically, many people object to any kind of change.

How you could address it: Resistance to change is not bad in itself: the people who are most affected by the change often have the best arguments against the change. It pays to listen to these objections. When moving forward and dealing with this issue, give people time to adjust and adapt. Stay in sync with the people involved. The personal transition and the inevitability of change based on economic drivers should become a part of the discussion: if something can be fully automated, it will be automated at some point in time. If your job is one that can be fully automated, it's time to learn a new skill anyway. Another viewpoint that will help is that some jobs will not change much, but are simply executed by another company (the cloud provider). As the cloud market matures, more services will be designed, bringing with it the need for analysts, developers, testers, *etc.* in the cloud provider's workforce.

Key takeaway: A very real risk for any change is the personal aspect: the people involved. If you use clear communication, set the right expectations and enable the personal transitions, the risk would be reduced, but it probably would not go away entirely.

7.17 Conclusion

When cloud does not offer the functionality you need, you will not move to cloud. When there is no business case or business rationale, you will not move to cloud. Like any technology, cloud alternatives need to be weighed for benefits, costs and risks. Make sure to do so with a long view, for that is when both the benefits and risks will become real. For now, if cloud is for you, it's ready to check the risks. Or if cloud is not for you, revisit the decision some time from now and see if the balance has tilted the other way.

Not to trumpet the writers' organization too much, but your channel partners and traditional service providers may add true value in the process by representing a broader view and sharing cross industry experiences.

A Measured Approach to Cloud Computing
Former CIO Emphasizes his
Realistic Expectations of Cloud

Hennie Wesseling hasn't bought the hype surrounding cloud computing, but he's hardly a skeptic. He's more of a cloud realist; in other words, he sees it as just one more tool in an IT executive's bag of tricks.

In Wesseling's eyes, the cloud at its best has become an attractive alternative to traditional IT strategies during times of financial strain, as well as an option for rolling out new IT services quickly and easily. But as any good realist would, he holds cloud computing to the same standards any other business tool needs to meet, refusing to charge ahead into it with blinders on.

Wesseling came to that outlook during the last few years of a 30-year stint at Dutch firm TNT N.V. that saw him eventually become CIO of the logistics company's mail division before leaving the company in early 2010. The last 18 months of his tenure coincided with the global economic crisis, and capital investment dollars were hard to come by. It was that economic reality that led Wesseling to take the mail division's first step into the cloud, entrusting the parcel services unit's CRM environment to software-as-a-service pioneer Salesforce.com.

When the move was met by immediate pushback from IT staff due to the company's SAP-centric strategy, Wesseling made it clear that he wasn't changing that strategy, but was rather just exploring his options. "I'm not saying that in the long run, this is the best way to do it," he says. "But I put a team on it, and I asked them to learn about the impact cloud computing would have on the company from a financial, legal and contract perspective."

Identifying Cloud's Unexpected Benefits—and its Potential Potholes

While Salesforce met all of Wesseling's core requirements—namely, low initial cost and quick deployment—he says its biggest payoff was of an unexpected variety. Facing new competitive pressure for the business of an important customer, SAP reacted quickly with alternative pricing and licensing models, once it got wind that the company was evaluating cloud alternatives. Add that to the list of things Wesseling finds the cloud useful for: as a bargaining chip.

But Wesseling's cloud-analysis team identified a few areas of serious concern that, to be frank, most other companies haven't considered. None of them are

131

scaring Wesseling off, but they've strengthened his resolve to ensure that cloud offerings fully meet all of the necessary business requirements.

For instance, the team pulled a random cloud computing contract from the Internet and studied it, finding a clause that said, effectively, if a client doesn't pay, the data becomes the property of the cloud provider. That clause, it turned out, was specific to the laws of the state of Texas in the U.S., where the vendor was based. It's a law that few European companies would have any reason to know, and its inclusion serves as an important reminder that the language of a provider's contract is critical to whether that provider is the right one to meet a company's cloud computing needs.

On a related front, the team was unable to find any contractual language covering what happens when a customer opts to transition from one provider to another. Wesseling says it would be crucial to get assurances in advance that a provider would be committed to providing the same level of service even if a customer was preparing to leave.

But the issue that really got Wesselings attention was the long-planned move from IPv4 to IPv6, a new Internet protocol whose main advantage is the addition of billions of IP addresses to accommodate the exponential growth of Internet-connected devices. According to Wesseling, most companies are shying from upgrading their applications and networks to support IPv6, a huge investment that delivers few immediate tangible benefits, bringing to mind the reluctance of many companies to adequately address the Y2K conundrum more than a decade ago.

Heading into Cloud with Eyes Wide Open is Critical

Wesseling finds it maddening that no one seems to grasp the impact a lack of IP addresses, insecure domain name servers, and growing routing problems in the transition from IPv4 to IPv6 will have on the ability to get the most out of cloud computing. In fact, he says it's reason enough for him to consider suggesting that any company should focus its cloud strategy on developing a private cloud, rather than relying on the Internet-based public cloud.

Wesseling, who continues to consult on IT issues, says the depletion of IP addresses at a time when so many business processes and so much data are being put into the cloud is similar to other resource issues businesses are facing.

"If I start a business that's dependent on oil even though there will be no oil next year, will any bank give me a loan?" he asks.

Despite the reality check such areas of concern provide, and the likelihood that it will be years before large companies are willing to place mission critical apps such as supply chain management in the cloud, Wesseling remains convinced that cloud computing holds immediate potential. But before he was going to let his company head down the path of entrusting what he calls "throw-away" applications—apps that are largely for the exchange of information internally, and without which the business could survive—to the cloud, he wanted to make sure the company understood the potential obstacles that might arise.

If he didn't take such steps, he insists, he'd be letting down the company he's served for so long.

"Stepping up to the cloud as a blind man is a bit foolish," says Wesseling. "I look at this from a business perspective, not an IT perspective. If I can't guarantee the basics to my company, I don't think I'm doing my job."

First Steps into Cloud Force Big Companies to Get Familiar with Technical, Legal and Compliance Risks

Commodity Trading Firm's Cloud Opportunity Introduced Complex Challenges

Figuring out that cloud computing might help your company is the beginning of a long journey. The cloud represents a new IT paradigm, one that requires new ways of thinking about data and the implications of its movement outside a company's firewalls. For large companies, this means delving into a process of inquiry and discovery, and that's just what one American commodity trading firm had to do.

The company in question, which requested anonymity in relaying its story, is in the process of replacing its ERP system, moving from a system running on an antiquated architecture to a thin-client application with a significant grid computing component. After looking at the product more closely, the IT team concluded that it presented an opportunity to use a public cloud provider to host the system's test and development environment. Doing so would allow the company to purchase fewer servers for the ERP system, quickly ramp computing capacity up and down to meet demand, and pay only for the capacity it needed rather than paying for servers to sit idle.

But there was a complex consideration: The test and development environment could contain transactional data on the trading of bulk commodities between buyers and sellers around the world. That meant data on those buyers and sellers might be crossing borders to be processed on servers in countries with differing privacy laws. It also meant that data could exist outside the company's immediate control.

"We knew it would work technologically, but from a compliance and legal perspective, there was a lot of work to do," says the company's IT director.

Discussion of Cloud Raises Serious Questions, Helps Get Answers

The IT team set up a meeting with the company's compliance staff, and started to explain the potential benefits and risks of a cloud-based test and development environment. "After the first 15 minutes, they all had glazed looks on their eyes, as if they had no idea what we were talking about," the IT director recalls.

Once it was made clear that the primary consideration was the movement of financial and contact information outside of the company's data centers, the questions started flowing. Is the network in question secure and encrypted? What kind of risks would the company face if its trading partners were identified? How do we know where the data is sitting? If another company using the same "cloud service" became involved in litigation, how would we know our data would be protected during the legal discovery process?

The company began talking to cloud providers to get answers, and it quickly crossed Google and others off the list because of their unwillingness to disclose the location of their data centers. Ultimately, the company went with Amazon Web Services' Elastic Compute Cloud, which allows customers to choose the geographic region of the data center where their information will be processed. The IT director got approval to run a portion of the company's test grid servers in an Amazon-hosted environment, and as of press time, he was still awaiting final approval to move data from there into the production environment.

Cloud Yields Benefits, But Legal Implications Lack Clarification

As for the performance of the test environment, it delivered classic cloud computing benefits. The company was getting 80% of the throughput of its old test environment, but rather than paying thousands up front for each server and hundreds each month for management and maintenance, it was instead spending 12 cents per hour on computing resources, and only when those resources were actually being used. The IT director estimates the costs at about $40 per month per server.

He also says the effort has yielded an important lesson—namely, that the compliance and legal implications of cloud computing are not well understood, nor are there sufficient laws and regulations to protect customers. The technology is solid, he says, but placing his company's core systems or sensitive data in the public cloud is simply not an option yet.

"From a security standpoint, it's probably more solid than what's in our data center," the IT director says. "The uncertainty comes from the 'what if?' Over the next year or two, some legal matter is going to prompt some laws and regulations in this space. Because of the lack of that today, it just makes us nervous."

His advice to other IT teams considering the cloud? Be sure you're aware of the risks you assume in an environment lacking clear oversight. "Before you go do anything," he says, "go talk to your legal and compliance groups."

8 Data: The New Frontier

8.1 Introduction

This book so far has described the phenomenon of cloud computing. This chapter moves somewhat beyond the cloud to focus on data, which is the functional essence of the cloud. Data is the new frontier, and something fundamentally new is happening to it. We are witnessing a movement away from raw data to intelligent or smart data, a movement rooted in the most nourishing of environments: the cloud. There data from different sources can combine and generate new information, in turn yielding fresh insights and business intelligence and creating valuable new products and services.

> As water droplets make up the real clouds in the sky, data is the critical component of the cloud in computing. And as with clouds in the sky, data clouds can range from single isolated ones to massive complex ones formed through the interactions of powerful internal and external forces.

8.2 Consumer Data in the Cloud

The web has undergone significant innovative and disruptive phases over the last 15 years. From the initial browser, e-commerce, and more recently the Web 2.0 phenomenon of mass participation in community-based social media sites, each phase has brought new challenges and opportunities. The movement of data into the cloud is one such phase offering both evolutionary and revolutionary opportunities to fundamentally change what we do with data and the way we think about data. Questions of ownership, management, distribution, control, and privacy of data will become challenging. This is already happening for a significant portion of web users. Social media users upload their profiles, social activities, and musings on to the web with a willing acceptance that ownership and privacy concerns are secondary to communication and connectedness. People gladly hand over their personal details to be able to play games or run a virtual farm on Facebook. Sometimes they don't even know that they have moved data from their digital devices such as phones and computers into the cloud. The services being consumed, and the types of data that are shared in the cloud are varied, which is evident in the range of sites/ companies shown in Figure 8.1 (Meeker *et al.* 2010).

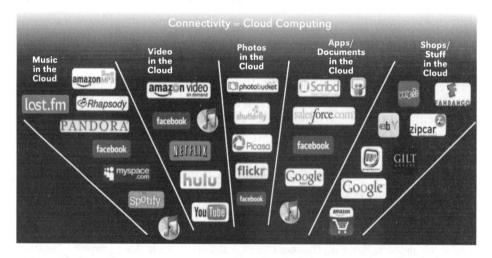

Figure 8.1: The cloud is everywhere today: the connected user can access a wide range of products and services on the cloud. The user can work, shop and be entertained from anywhere—a paradise for some! (Copyright 2010 Morgan Stanley)

Being able to see and follow activity within a network of friends has helped drive a greater demand for transparency all round, particularly in the US. Citizens demand insight into government activities and especially into how their taxes are being spent. Similarly, these groups of connected users, marking a new generation of workers, expect connectedness amongst their peers as a workplace norm. This in turn has encouraged some C-level executives to experiment with and learn from new methods of managing and controlling data flow, both inside and outside of their organization, to foster an environment where serendipity and good discovery become the norm.

8.3 Change in Mindset

Conceptually cloud computing has done away with the need for physical ownership of computing resources. It also challenges the orthodoxy of the traditional IT command and control model. Cloud computing enables the decoupling of applications from infrastructure, of data from infrastructure and applications, and even of data from the organization. The challenge now is to leverage this change in mindset to maximize the potential of data in the cloud.

Large amounts of consumer opinions on products and services are being willingly offered and published by consumers themselves on social networking sites. These comments are becoming a treasure trove of business intelligence providing market insights into consumer behavior. They are being used to great effect by companies such as Ford Motor Company, PepsiCo, and Southwest Airlines, to name but a few (Bughin 2010). This group of active consumers has driven the *first wave* of data in the cloud.

Governments are behind the *second wave*, offering their data more or less unencumbered in the cloud, thereby giving companies and in particular startups and active citizens the opportunity to exploit it for their own advantage. Some companies are already leveraging data currently available in the cloud. More will do so to complement their own internal information systems.

The opportunity now exists for companies to experiment with placing some or all of their own data in the cloud, where it will meld with other data there and be used by others in different, perhaps even unexpected and unimagined ways. Business data in the cloud will form the *third wave*.

The movement of data into the cloud has started. It is likely that large amounts of data from governments, non-governmental organizations (NGOs), corporations, commercial information providers and web users will become available through the cloud. We can expect that there will be many interesting opportunities to participate in making data available in the cloud and harnessing other data there.

8.4   Data Evolution

The Internet is pervasive and is connecting, creating, transporting, and consuming ferocious amounts of data from increasingly diverse sources including mobile phones, RFID (radio frequency identification) tags, sensors, healthcare, financial services, and social networking environments. It is estimated that the amount of data on networks will triple by 2014 from today's volume, as shown in Cisco's Visual Networking Index (VNI) in Figure 8.2 (see Cisco in the References section of this book). This explosive growth will then be equivalent to moving approximately 14 billion DVDs over the network every month (Miller 2010).

These enormous amounts of data support the metaphor of data being the lifeblood of the Internet. Data is critical to the effective functioning of every modern person and organization. This is evidenced by what has been achieved over the last 15 years on the web.

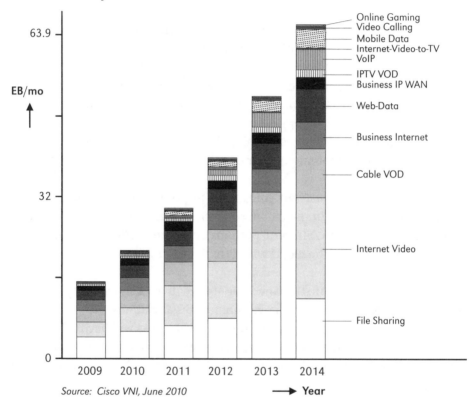

Figure 8.2: Cisco's Visual Networking Index (VNI) charts the explosive growth in data and breaks down the data types

The initial web—Web 0—saw the launch and commercialization of the browser and the birth of Netscape and the subsequent browser wars. This profession-alized the *publication* and sharing of material on the web. This was transformational: the dynamic of content being easily viewed by many rather than a few. Commercial transactions and new types of business then evolved on the web. This phase—Web 1.0—saw companies like eBay, Amazon, and Google define and dominate the web.

The next phase—Web 2.0—sees the advent of *participation* and engagement where users actively engage and communicate with each other. Web 2.0 and social media have become synonymous (Bloem 2009). Companies like Facebook, Twitter and Apple are currently driving this era of the web. It also marks a movement towards a plethora of device types that are used to create and consume content: the PC, phone, console, TV, and tablet. The movement from *publication* to *participation* has again been transformative. The potential of true participation and its impact on society, governments, and business is only starting to be realized. Participation is as significant an event as the original browser, according to the distinguished scholar Professor Larry Prusak (see Prusak's URL in the References section of this book).

Yet despite all of the advances in the web, which we now take for granted, the underlying data that drive and enable each of the phases of the web hasn't changed much. Though it has transformed enormously in terms of volume over the years, data at its core has not changed much. All of the complexity and increased functionality of use has been achieved through multiple waves of innovation. More complex and faster computers, routers, and networks have helped create better technologies, methods, algorithms, and applications with the many acronyms that are shown in Figure 8.3 (Hawke 2010; Linked Data 2010). These have helped deliver today's web but mask the underlying rawness of the core data. At issue is the difficulty computer technology has in intelligently understanding data: a router knows the destination of a packet but not its content; a search query will return a result without knowing the meaning of the words in the query result.

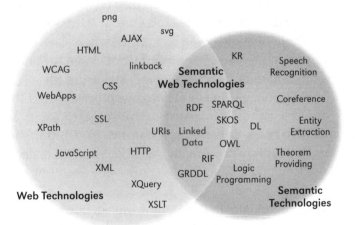

Figure 8.3: Linked data leverages the best of today's web technology and is the forefront of creating a smart data environment

8.5 Dumb versus Smart Data

The data underpinning the web today can be characterized as "dumb." Computers don't know the meaning of the text forming the web pages we read. The innovation challenge now is to make the data "smart." With such data, computer technology can infer meaning and do smart things with it. If we realize that all of the successes of the web to date have been achieved on "dumb" data, we can barely imagine what will be possible with "smart" data. Up till now, the perception of smartness has been achieved by applications performing more clever extraction, transformation and load functions (ETL) to create and deliver the right information.

One of the most endearing features of the web is its ease of use and lack of formal structure. Text is relatively easy to input and publish. Humans automatically know how to read, interpret, and understand the meaning and context of text data on the web: converting raw text into coherent and readable stories. Computers, on the other hand, cannot easily complete the same task. Without structure, computers are at a loss—they suffer from a text problem. As most of the web is created using unstructured text, the challenge is to create structure without constraining the ability to easily input and publish. Add to this the enormous amount of unstructured data that is already in an enterprise, from emails, marketing material, customer information and feedback, and the potential challenges ahead are daunting.

Significant advances have been made to create smart data and put structure around unstructured text. The most theoretically smart data being researched focuses on the *semantic web* and is often referred to as the "Web 3.0." Sir Tim Berners-Lee first proposed the semantic web in 2001 (Berners-Lee *et al.* 2001). It is a natural extension of the current web and it anticipates a future where computers will (semi-) automatically understand data using advances in fields such as artificial intelligence (AI), natural language processing (NLP), ontologies, linguistics, and reasoning. It is a very active research topic: at DERI, the largest semantic web research center in the world (see DERI in the References section of this book), there are already over 130 researchers dedicated to this topic alone.

The semantic web is a web where data and content is linked, in contrast to today's web of linked pages and hyperlinks. It is a web understood by both humans and computers alike. While the realization of this vision may be some

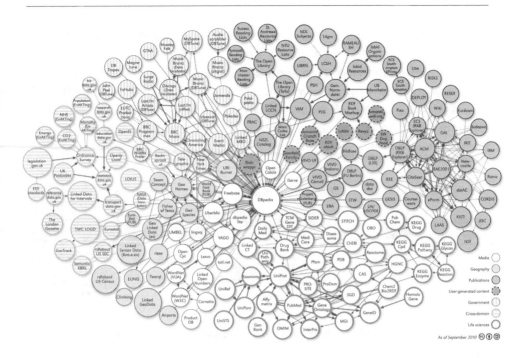

Figure 8.4: Linked data is represented by a graph. Once you enter the graph you can traverse it and access any information attached (Cyganiak and Jentzsch 2010)

time off, the *first instance* of structured smart data is already being created and made available in the cloud. The first version of this smart data is called "linked data" and sits in the middle between the existing web and the semantic web (as illustrated in Figure 8.3). The set of linked data is growing all the time. A snapshot view of it is shown in Figure 8.4 (W3C-SWEO 2010): the diagram shows a high-level relationship diagram of the different data domains that are currently available, and where the links exist between these domains.

For example, the geographic references in the DBpedia data set (which is essentially Wikipedia in a more structured form; see DBpedia in the References section of this book) are linked to the GeoNames data set, which in turn is linked to and from many other data sets such as US Census data (see Figure 8.4). Once a data set is linked into the cloud, it is possible to navigate across, access, and link each of the other data sets. Therefore, an application that references a city, for example, can automatically access available information about the city from linked data sources in the cloud, such as the CIA's *Factbook* (see CIA in the References section of this book).

Putting data in the cloud in its current "dumb" state is limiting in its potential. However, exposing data in a linked, smart format in the cloud is different, potentially ground breaking, and powerful. It benefits from the network effect as described metaphorically by Metcalfe's law and illustrated in Figure 8.5 (see Wikipedia in the References section of this book). Linked data benefits from the addition of new users to populate the network, much as the telephone network grew.

Figure 8.5: Linked Data benefits from being connected as the telephone did with the addition of new users. Metcalfe's law applies

The network effect will be achieved most when all linked data is exposed to and accessible throughout the cloud. We have already seen the benefits from linking computers and users, and now it is time to take advantage of linking and connecting data.

8.6 Data in the Cloud

Several ingenious cases are emerging that exemplify the potential of linked data for organizations. These cases cross several sectors including life sciences, government, and media.

A life science example

Linking Open Drug Data (LODD) is an initiative of the Health Care and Life Sciences Interest Group of the W3C to create open linked data about drugs. The sources of data range from information about the impacts of drugs on gene expression to clinical trial results. Approximately 370,000 links to external data sources are contained in the LODD data sets (see Figure 8.6 (W3C-HCLSIG 2010)). One interesting case demonstrated how users find information on the effect of Chinese herbs on particular diseases. The users can also find relevant clinical trial information, active ingredients, and any reported side effects. The data has also been used to help medical researchers investigate genes of herbs and how they could help in specific diseases (Jentzsch 2009).

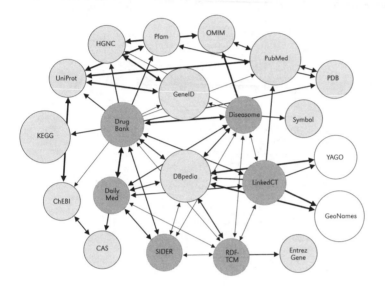

Figure 8.6: Linking open drug data

A government example

High-profile initiatives, like the US government's effort to make its data more accessible, have helped greatly in making massive amounts of linked data available in the cloud. Data.gov is the site to access this data, and it has a stated purpose to democratize public-sector data and drive innovation. One year after its launch it has helped create a community around open linked data that includes 6 countries establishing open linked data initiatives (including Britain and Canada), 8 US states offering data sites, 8 cities in America with open data, and approximately 275,000 data sets being made available (see Data-Gov-A in the References section of this book). Some of these data sets are illustrated in Figure 8.7 (Li and Hendler 2009).

145

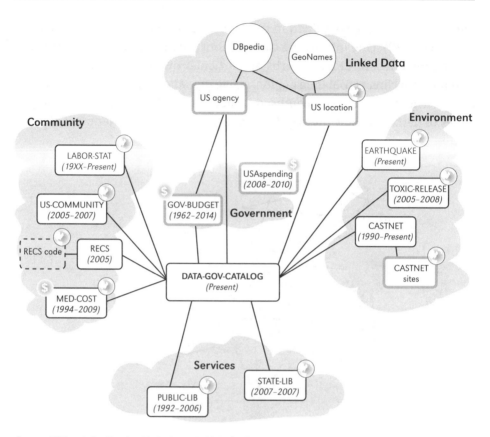

Source: Li Ding & Jim Hender, 'Tetherless World Constellation',
Rensselaer Polytechnic Institute, data-gov.tw.rpi.edu, Oct 2009

Figure 8.7: The breadth and depth of available and accessible government data
is enormous. Its utility is greatly increased when accessible in linked format and
connected to other open and linked data sources.

It is a great example of where the old adage of "build it and they will come"
actually works. Some very interesting and diverse uses are being created
using this data. One such use is shown in Figure 8.8, which charts the percentage of cancelled or diverted flights by destination (see Fly on Time in the
References section of this book).

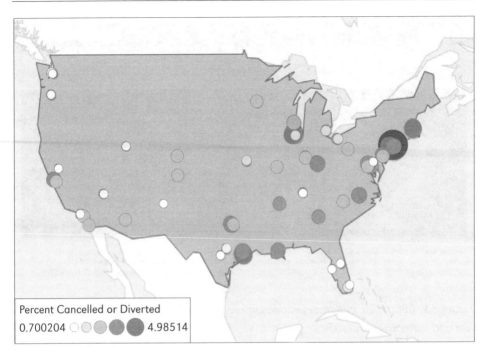

Figure 8.8: The percentage of cancelled or delayed flights by destination, based on US government open linked data

A media example

The BBC created a new music web site that reuses linked data from MusicBrainz and Wikipedia to help it deliver an enhanced and differentiating service. A snapshot of the site is shown in Figure 8.9 (see BBC Music in the References section of this book). Matthew Shorter, interactive editor of music at the BBC, puts forward three arguments for using linked data (Blumauer 2009B, Ferguson 2009):

1. Reuse: BBC avoids wasting money in creating data that is already available in the public domain through MusicBrainz and Wikipedia.
2. Search Engine Optimization (SEO): more meaningful linkages between data yields better search retrieval of content.
3. Open Platform: a better user experience means extended session times. It also increases the likelihood that other users will access the site and bring their music links with them, thereby extending its reach and value to all users.

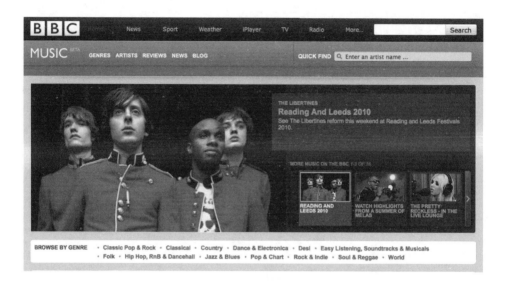

Figure 8.9: BBC music integrates various linked data music sources to create a richer site and better user experience

8.7 Tapping into the Data Potential for Organizations

As the previous examples show, the real value of linked data lies in the actual links. These links can be exploited to access information, enabling organizations to experiment, evaluate, and innovate with new sources and types of information. As with any type of new initiative, business executives will be looking for a clear business rationale to justify the expenditure and define the benefits. These benefits could be for the organization itself, but could also be a contribution to the organization's ecosystem, where collaboration is taking place. For governments and NGOs the incremental cost of exposing already existing information to the cloud in linked-data format can be defended in terms of serving and benefiting the common good. For most commercial organizations, open linked data as a full-on business proposition is a long way off. In addition, companies cannot contemplate moving mission-critical information systems until the technology creating linked data is more robust and mature. At the moment, most data that resides in organizations' private clouds or inside traditional platforms does not have enough classification information in it to allow easy distinction between the data you would and would not want to share.

In an interview, Prof. Dr. Chris Bizer, the force behind DBpedia, suggested that publically available linked data could be used by organizations as a data back-drop to augment corporate data. This augmentation can be achieved in an experimental manner and quickly develop and grow into a more robust deployed application. Most critically this can be achieved without radically changing the corporate applications or data sets. In the same interview, he suggested that linked data could be used as a lightweight data-integration technology.

This approach is incremental and experimental, but avoids the big upfront investment required in modeling global schemas used in classic data-ware-housing projects (Blumauer 2009A).

As of April 2010, the DBpedia dataset describes more than 3.4 million things, out of which 1.5 million are classified in a consistent manner, including 312,000 persons, 413,000 places, 94,000 music albums, 49,000 films, 15,000 video games,  140,000 organizations, 146,000 species and 4,600 diseases. The data set features labels and abstracts for these 3 million-odd things in up to 92 different languages; 1,460,000 links to images and 5,543,000 links to external web pages; 4,887,000 external links into other RDF datasets, 565,000 Wikipedia categories, and 75,000 YAGO categories. (see Wikipedia in the References section of this book).

At the Semantic Technology 2010 conference, linked data was described as a viable means of augmenting corporate data and creating better information for applications in financial services. Sample applications include (Semantic Universe 2010):

- Mergers and acquisitions.
- Anti-money laundering.
- Anti-counterfeiting.
- Customer and market analysis.
- Business intelligence.

Like many large data sets, linked data needs to be sourced, cleansed, pack-aged, and of good enough quality and accuracy to be of use to organizations. Maintaining or verifying it might be done by corporations themselves, but can also be taken on by third parties. Real value and intellectual property (IP) can be created from this type of data, which creates new business opportunities for the companies themselves, incumbent information providers and start-ups alike.

8.8   **Challenges**

As with any technology or phenomenon that is new and evolving, linked data in the cloud introduces a whole raft of new concerns for C-level executives. These concerns need to be examined before taking big steps in sharing data publicly or using someone else's data. The challenges can be grouped into three sections: legal, data, and technology.

As linked data itself is new and evolving, *legal* opinions are also entering new and uncharted territories. Principal amongst these is that actual ownership, location, and consumption of data may reside simultaneously in different jurisdictions with conflicting regulatory, legal, IP, and privacy requirements. Established governance, regulatory, and legal frameworks may also not be appropriate. As computers can infer meaning from linked data, possibly misleading or untrue statements could be created, leading to all sorts of potential legal problems (Harley *et al.* 2009). At the same time, the regulatory and legal frameworks that are currently in place are probably not yet ready to cover large-scale adoption and use of linked data by organizations. This too will add to the legal concerns. However, innovative technology solutions and the necessities of businesses to innovate and participate in this space will help replace legal uncertainty with legal clarity. It only takes a few pioneers to lead the way, greatly helping other organizations' adoption.

From a *data* perspective several interesting issues arise, some of which also hold true for more traditional data sources. They include:
- Attributing authorship of original and derivative data.
- Knowing the quality and the accuracy of the data and its source.
- Dealing with data duplication and disambiguation (resolving conflicts in meaning).
- Identifying data source and lineage (or *provenance*) and knowing the retention requirements for difference types of data across various jurisdictions.

A recent Pew Research Center report expressed wariness about further exposing private information to governments, corporations, thieves, opportunists, and human and machine error (Anderson and Rainie 2010). A lot of these issues are evolving in the social media space and solutions to most of these issues are being created as they arise.

When it comes to analyzing data, companies like Google handle text differently from most organizations. Traditional web development environments (for example, LAMP: Linux, Apache, MySQL, and PHP) find it difficult to scale and process large volumes of data. Newer technologies (like Hadoop and NoSQL) are becoming available to overcome these difficulties. Acquiring the competencies to use these new and emerging technologies will take time, and these skills will initially be scarce.

Hadoop is a software framework that enables applications to work with thousands of nodes and massive amounts of data.

NoSQLs are next generation databases that are non-relational, distributed and scalable. MongoDB is one such database.

Additional *technical* complexities arise in creating, curating and provisioning data if real-time access to information is required, such as in financial services and new media. Latency or lack of bandwidth can also be a problem, depending on particular business and data needs. As new requirements and demands are being created, new technologies will be developed to satisfy these needs. Technological obsolescence is therefore a problem.

8.9   Conclusion

Something new is afoot regarding data. Gone are the days of data created in a manner that renders it "dumb" and non-intelligent to computers. Making data "smart" is the next big thing—the new frontier. Computers can discover, interpret, and manipulate data and infer meaning with smart data, and linked data is a first step in this direction. Governments are in a first wave that aims to make data more accessible to citizens and commercial entities. Industry is following, with news media and life sciences in particular showing some early promise. Other industries are closely behind. Linked data affords organizations the opportunity to look at and exploit data differently; decoupled from technology, applications, and indeed the organization itself, it offers a cost-effective way to experiment with diverse data sources. These sources can be private, partner, public domain, or third-party information providers. Linked data presents the opportunity to truly tap into a vast resource of data and convert it into real information and knowledge. Companies that plan for and innovate around this new type of data will engage with their customers, partners, and competitors differently and will bring new types of product and services to market faster. Data is innovation. Data is the new frontier.

Transformation Specialist Helps Reinier de Graaf Groep Find its Way in the Cloud
Fresh Perspective Leads Hospital Group's Move into Cloud Computing

It's no wonder that many IT executives drag their feet on cloud computing; it's a whole new computing paradigm that requires them to look at their jobs—and at IT as a whole—from a totally different perspective. That can be a significant challenge in the context of daily work responsibilities, which is why sometimes the impetus to consider something new like cloud computing requires just that: a fresh perspective.

Reinier de Graaf Groep, the oldest hospital group in The Netherlands, with 500 beds at 6 hospitals in the western region of the country, has learned this first hand. The company recently wrapped up a nearly two-year period in which Ben Gorter, an IT transition specialist, served as acting CIO overseeing the transformation of an IT department that had become a serious handicap. Perhaps the most important tool Gorter relied upon to engineer that transition was a concept that had been totally foreign to the Reinier de Graaf, namely the cloud.

Gorter says that when he arrived on the scene in late 2008, there was a litany of problems. A lack of capital investment in IT had resulted in an operation saddled with aging, obsolete equipment. The IT staff had been whittled down to a skeleton crew that lacked the knowledge needed to run a hospital IT environment. Worse yet, Reinier de Graaf was spending just 2.1 percent of its budget on IT, far below industry norms.

Gorter was able to tackle the last issue by convincing hospital leadership to pump up IT spending to 4.5 percent of the budget, and he's been assured that will rise to closer to 6 percent in the future. Capital investment dollars remained scarce, however, and Gorter decided to wait on bolstering the staff until he had a clear idea of what was needed. He began to look at applications, and quickly identified his first priority: The hospital's email system was in dire need of replacement. Given the limited capital available, he suggested that a cloud solution would be cheaper, easier and—most importantly—faster to deploy. And this was coming from a then-self-avowed cloud computing skeptic.

"Initially, I was not so convinced that the cloud was going to have a huge impact," he says. "But now, I think it will have a very large impact on IT and delivery."

Initial Cloud Success Provides Momentum for Further Efforts

Gorter's confidence in the cloud was buoyed by the subsequent success of the cloud-based Microsoft Exchange environment adopted by Reinier de Graaf. That service, hosted by a Microsoft partner, proved to be even more efficient, dependable and available than was hoped, and it emboldened Gorter to make the cloud a larger part of Reinier de Graaf's ongoing implementation of his IT transformation plan.

The move toward the cloud is progressing to a more comprehensive Microsoft-centric strategy in which the software giant itself will take over hosting of the hospital's Exchange environment and combine that with cloud-based instances of SharePoint (collaboration), Office Communication Server (presence) and Live-Meeting (web conferencing).

Gorter also has spurred Reinier de Graaf to entrust its hardware and services to an unidentified infrastructure-as-a-service provider, a transition that was set to occur by the end of 2010, and is expected to yield a vastly improved computing capacity at a low up-front cost and with minimal staffing requirements. It also will give the hospital a lot of flexibility to scale its resources up or down should it decide to merge with another hospital, Gorter says.

But such a move is no small consideration when patient data is at issue. That's why hospital leaders brought in consultants from Ernst & Young to advise them on the contract specifics they'd need to guarantee that patients' privacy would be adequately protected.

Going forward, Gorter foresees additional opportunities for Reinier de Graaf to tap the cloud, most notably for systems management tools, ERP components such as financials and human resources, and even X-ray systems. (Conversely, he says, hospital systems that contain personal health records won't go the cloud route any time soon.)

Big Change Brings Pain, But Also Quick Results

All of the benefits aside, Reinier de Graaf's cloud strategy hasn't been without its opponents. In fact, Gorter says that a full one-third of the hospital's IT department has left due to not wanting to be part of the transition. And those who have stayed have struggled in adapting to a new protocol-intensive approach to IT that allows for less improvisation and independence.

"It's a very predictable way of working, but IT people have to follow the rules," says Gorter. "It's not their best competence, and that's one of the competencies we're looking for: You have to follow rules."

While a rule-oriented cloud environment may not make for an attractive job listing, it does significantly speed up the process of transforming an IT operation, and that was Gorter's primary goal. He says other IT executives engineering IT transformations would be wise to piggyback on his experience.

"Cloud computing is an opportunity. You can build things on your own, you can buy things on your own, or you can buy services from cloud providers," says Gorter. "When you want to make a transition very fast, when your problems are very large and very difficult and you need to move quickly, it's an opportunity you should consider."

Strong words from a former cloud skeptic.

9 Creating Your Roadmap

9.1 Introduction

Throughout this book, we have seen that adopting cloud computing is not only a technological change, but that it has a far-reaching impact. Signposts like business technology, new ways of (self) provisioning and the importance of enterprise architecture can be found throughout the previous chapters. In this final chapter, we'll survey and add directions and concrete suggestions that will help you take the next step. The chapter will help you build your roadmap to the cloud.

Of course, *the one* universal roadmap for cloud computing does not exist. The exact steps you will take all depend on your organization, your goals and, to a lesser extent, on your current technology. Even the order in which to take the steps may be different from organization to organization. One might choose to start with server virtualization as a step to more responsive IT, where another might jump ahead by signing up for Salesforce.com. Some might choose to quickly embrace cloud as the default option, while others will use it sparingly where risks are low and return almost immediate.

Where to start

As long as the considerations around cloud computing remain abstract, it is very hard to define any action or even quantify its real value. Early on, you should make an effort to discuss some specific applications of cloud computing, cloud services or even the separate concepts that make up cloud. For example, you could examine virtualization or chargeback on its own, to see if it makes business sense to adopt it. Or you could look into the specific opportunities for embracing web-based email. At the same time, keep an eye on the bigger transformation towards cloud that is taking place, too.

When cloud computing is embraced in its entirety, there will be new initiatives across the whole organization: there will be activities to change IT, activities to bring change to the business side and, most of all, there will be changes to the interaction and collaboration between business and IT.

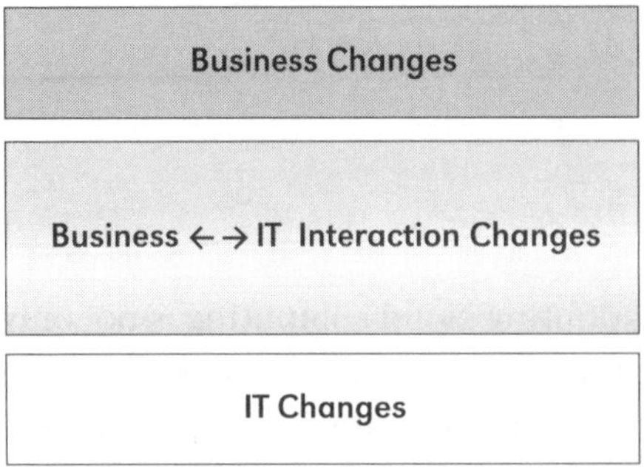

Figure 9.1: Changes due to cloud computing

In the ideal world, you would take steps towards cloud computing in all areas simultaneously, right from the start. Ideally, business and technology will work closely together to craft a new way of leveraging technology in business. It is the best way to build the readiness and skills needed. More flexible IT without a business process to apply it will not produce the desired business agility. Or, vice versa, business users who are self-provisioning their IT from the cloud but do not interact with the IT team will ultimately run into trouble. Reality in your organization may dictate that one of these areas has to be addressed first, but activities in the other areas should follow shortly thereafter.

9.2 Business Changes Toward Cloud Computing

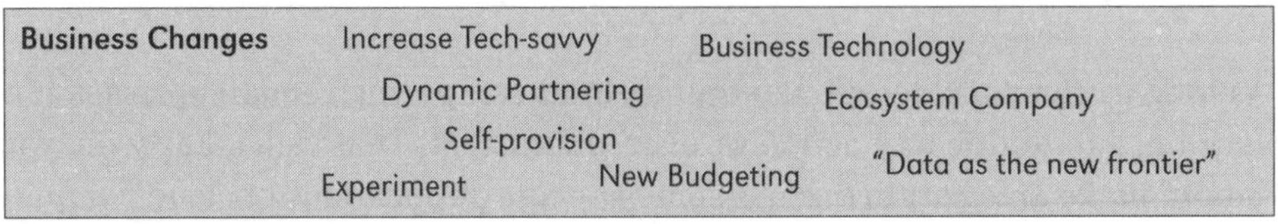

Figure 9.2: Business changes due to cloud computing

As discussed in Chapter 3, information technology is changing into business technology. In organizations that fully realize the role and importance of IT, the business side of the organization takes control and is becoming more tech savvy. This does not happen automatically, and requires the initiation of some new processes or one-time activities.

The activities that help the business adopt cloud computing are:

Experiment and examine current "rogue" cloud usage

It is quite possible that there is already rogue cloud IT in the organization. For example, users may have found an online tool that suits their needs for one particular process. This would be a good starting point to help the business understand the complete reality of using cloud resources: the benefits and the issues. If there is very little or no use of cloud services yet, you can initiate some experimentation on the business side. For example, try some new tools for marketing, project support or communication (yammer.com or IBM Lotus Live come to mind). This way, some business users will get the experience of choosing and signing up for their own IT, and will learn the issues that come with it. In the process, they may actually find some business relevant services that they want to keep for real!

Increase technological savvy

A longer-term strategy will be increasing the technology skills of business executives. Perhaps taking a well-known piece of technology like the smartphone as a starting point, the discussion should encompass the reality of connecting to other companies through technology, user-driven innovation and the role digital services play in the core products and processes of the company. Establish a *"digital first"* vision that describes how the digital realm will be used to be competitive and customer oriented. The goal here is not to train executives in the finer details of database construction, but the overall concepts of strategy for and with technology should be clear.

Reconsider budgeting practices

When IT conforms more to the pay-per-use model, the business budgeting should change accordingly. After cloud computing starts to gain some momentum, the practices around budgeting and financial management as a whole should be ready for a model where costs are calculated per transaction, per user or whichever granularity is relevant for the business. Make special note of the upward flexibility in case of unexpected success: if for example there is a sudden increase in the number of orders placed, the overall cost of IT will increase accordingly. In that case "breaking" the budget would be good!

Other activities

Extending the discussion around business intelligence, the business plans and ambitions should start to take into account the value and potential of data inside and outside the company. As discussed in Chapter 8, sharing data and using shared data is growing fast, and the organizations that will benefit most are the ones that learn fast and use the data to their benefit. Discover hidden value by finding out which data could actually be valuable to others, and figure out which partners could have data that would improve your own processes or decisions. This could be one step on the path to becoming an organization that is turning into an ecosystem player, using other parties to help create the end experience, product or service best and most efficiently.

9.3   Addressing the Business-IT Interaction

Business ← → IT Interaction Changes	Enterprise Architecture	
	Evaluate Value	Services Portfolio
	Business-IT Strategy	Innovation Committee

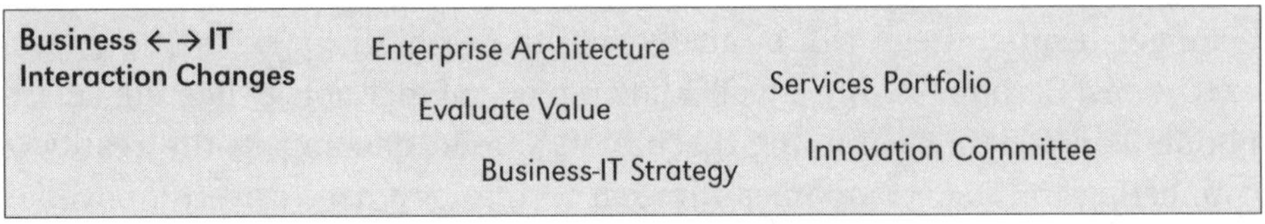

Figure 9.3: Business-IT interaction changes due to cloud computing

As we discussed in several of the previous chapters, the interaction between business and IT is an area where many developments occur as you're adopting cloud computing. The most important interactions of enterprise architects take place in this area, and this is where the strategic decisions for IT are being made. In this strategic dialogue long-term and short-term considerations need to be addressed and here you sort the standard, infrastructural elements of the business from the unique, innovative and competitive parts.

There are several activities you can undertake to improve the business-IT relationship while discovering the opportunities of cloud computing:

Do a joint discovery exercise

Let a group of IT and business people meet face-to-face and discuss your business drivers and how the different new IT developments can help. In a workshop format, a shared vision can be created that gives a clear direction and prioritization of possible options. Areas where cloud could be valuable and viable can be identified, and usually a workshop like this is a great opportunity to tighten the relations between business and IT people. Such a workshop is valuable for alignment around any IT innovation, but especially in the case of cloud computing.

The real business drivers are sometimes surprisingly hard to find or formulate on the spot, so some preparation is needed here. Also, the IT people should be prepared to present the different elements of cloud, as they can be valuable to business. In most cases, some related technologies are included, too: for example, mobile computing or web technology in general. This exercise is often done with help from external consultants who do the workshop preparation, moderation and reporting,[*] but it can also be executed completely by your own team.

This discovery exercise might include, after discussing the business drivers, presenting a range of cloud services, introducing them briefly and seeing how they can match up with the business drivers. It could be the first step to the creation of a cloud portfolio.

Create the business case

After finding some areas where cloud computing might be useful, a business case can be made. In some instances it will be fairly straightforward to calculate costs and returns, while in other cases the best you can do is establish a rationale or vision as to how cloud would be valuable. If no hard ROI can be proven, it does not necessarily mean no ROI will be attained in the end. It may be a business decision to invest in an area that looks promising, but currently is not mature enough for a solid business case: perhaps adopting an industry-specific cloud solution or choosing a relatively new startup company to provide business process integration online.

---

[*] Sogeti offers this service under the name of TechnoVision™ (Hessler).

An easy business case can be calculated for things that are more or less standardized: virtualization as part of your private cloud initiatives, email in the cloud or collaborative platforms in the cloud. Weighing cost, benefits, opportunities and risks of a traditional solution against the cloud solution should give a good indication whether cloud, in this situation, is the smart thing to do. As mentioned before, in the case of a pay-per use service, these calculations need to have some scenario-planning variables in them, too. What will happen over time, and how would that change the outcome of your comparison? Finally, even though these business cases are relatively straightforward, unless you have a real understanding of your current costs of operations, housing, power, people, recruitment, *etc.*, and also the value of your current level of quality, support and IT dedication, it will be hard to make a fair comparison. In the case of a new solution, these comparisons will be easier than in the case of migrating existing systems or infrastructure. When you are looking for an easy project to start, a new application is therefore the preferred option.

Find your entry point and potential quick wins

An important part of the dialogue between business and IT should address what is a good way to get started with cloud? Which project will you start with? Naturally, you will look for something that is not too large and complex, that demonstrates the value of cloud computing, and that can create some visibility inside the organization. You have the choice of starting in the public cloud, "outside in," or starting with the private cloud, "inside out." Quite a few private cloud projects primarily aim at reducing costs and improving the agility of internal IT, but do not aim to offer new functionality. As a result, the business visibility could be less than what would be achieved with a more functionally oriented public cloud project. Still, some private cloud projects will offer new and highly desirable features to the business. Examples are data mining, analytics or searches.

If you are really looking for innovation and want to experience the collaborative and connected nature of some cloud solutions, you could look for an internal system that is most related to one or more of your important trading partners and look for a cloud solution that could enhance the process: for example, by increasing automation, providing better information, bringing together multiple parties, offering better functionality and lowering costs for both parties, *etc.*

At IBM, workloads have been identified that offer the most favorable entry points for public and for private cloud delivery models (IBM 2010). These workloads are based on the analysis of study data and experience with actual cloud implementations. For organizations interested in piloting a public cloud service, the workloads listed in Table 9.1 are the projects that would likely pose the lowest risk and offer highest potential return. The same holds true for the workloads listed as top candidates for private cloud implementation.

Public cloud entry points	Private cloud entry points
Audio/video/web conferencing	Data mining, text mining, or other analytics
Webhosting	Data warehouses or data marts
Test environment infrastructure	Test environment infrastructure
VoIP Infrastructure	Business continuity and disaster recovery
Variable storage	Developer platforms
Software as a service	Long-term data archiving/preservation

Table 9.1: Workload recommendations

Not everything is suited for the cloud yet. Mission-critical applications, highly sensitive data workloads (such as employee and healthcare records), multiple codependent services (such as high throughput online transaction processing) and workloads requiring a high level of auditability and accountability (such as those subject to Sarbanes-Oxley) are not the preferred entry points for cloud computing (IBM Smart Business 2010).

Create a continuous innovation process

A joint discovery workshop is a good start, but even better would be to have a continuous dialogue about the company, strategy, projects, IT strategy *etc*. This strategic dialogue can have many forms. It can be embedded in frequent individual contacts between many different people, or it can take the form of regular meetings of an "innovation board." There could be online support tools, collaboration spaces and even crowdsourcing initiatives where a large number of people are invited to think about innovation and strategy. By including IT in this process, the organization will come closer to the business technology ideal and be better positioned to take advantage of new technology first. What would you have done if the iPad had been on your horizon from the day it was announced? Could you have created an app or complete application that would have used the mobile, connected, location-aware, personal nature of this new computing device? The same goes for many upcoming cloud services: if you are the first to use them, you'll have an advantage, provided you can weed out the ones that are not going to make it.

Looking at how and where cloud can be useful is not a one-time exercise. Your enterprise IT strategy will continuously redefine where the boundary between internal and cloud lies. Over the years, new developments will keep changing that boundary. Things that were too costly to move to the cloud will have become cheaper, applications that were once deemed unfit for cloud may find a good cloud alternative, and concerns that cannot be addressed today may no longer be problems for new services or service providers. All of this can be part of the innovation process, or the enterprise architecture dialogue; probably they are one and the same, since the people who would be involved in innovation are the same people who would be involved in enterprise architecture.

If your company is not ready for any of this, the easy low-key start would be for the CIO and enterprise architects to occasionally invite someone from the business for a one-on-one lunch or late-afternoon casual brainstorm on how IT could ideally be used in your organization. This would build a network of supporters who could, in a later stage, help bring about change.

Use enterprise architecture from the start

Cloud computing has the inherent risk of losing control. As mentioned in Chapter 6, this is not a bad thing, as long as the risk is an informed one and the biggest risks are countered by some preventive measures. Long-term and short-term success are not opposites, but it takes careful maneuvering to achieve both.

Enterprise architecture is essential in guiding the development of the IT landscape when implementing cloud solutions and making sure the technology is continuously in line with the business drivers (see Chapter 6). EA makes it possible to define the functionality, the quality and the structure of solutions, regardless of the manner of implementation. From this perspective, the technical implementation of these solutions is guided by the oversight that is needed when the components that realize those solutions can reside everywhere. To apply enterprise architecture well in the case of cloud computing, the following activities are relevant:

1. Reverse architecture the existing landscape, in order to discover the services and patterns in use by the organization and the variants of these services and patterns deployed.

2. Define the future state (to be) of services and patterns that are eligible for (partial) cloud implementation and realization. For every feasible scenario, an architectural study and impact analysis should be provided, using pattern variants as an outline to define and construct these artifacts.

3. Establish which deployment options are optimal, appointing feasible cloud candidates for delivery of services involved. This is based on a cloud classification approach that weighs the business value and commodity factor of each pattern and/or service variant. This step should be carried out in tandem with establishing the service portfolio and mapping the business capabilities onto services.

4. Guide the composition of request for proposals by providing functional descriptions of each pattern and service variant that is a cloud candidate. This description should contain:
   - A definition of functionality;
   - Purpose and goal of the variant;
   - Additional characteristics;
   - Quality aspects to be met; and
   - Implementation guidelines and standards that are important for integration of this functionality within the IT landscape as a whole.

5. Provide the same descriptions for services and patterns that remain the responsibility of the organization, but are affected by the deployment of facilities in the cloud. This provides a full overview of the changes that take place when implementing cloud services.

6. Guide the implementation, testing and deployment of cloud services and the (re)design and testing of internal facilities that are affected by cloud implementation.

If you have no mature enterprise architecture practice, establishing one would be recommended for many reasons, and especially for making cloud computing a success.

9.4   Getting IT Ready for Cloud

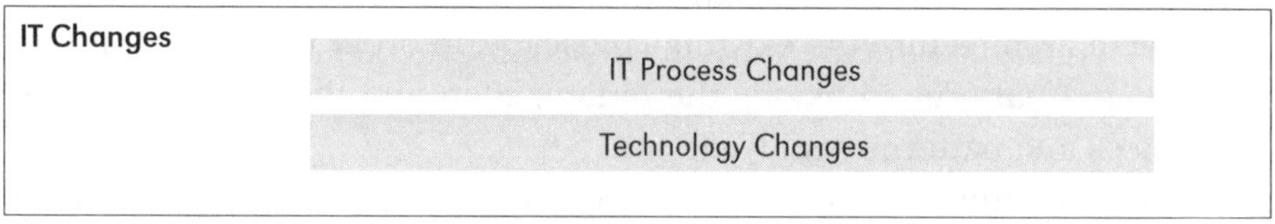

IT Changes	
	IT Process Changes
	Technology Changes

Figure 9.4: IT changes due to cloud computing

In the IT department, cloud computing has two distinct areas of impact: one is the technology itself, what technology we use and how it integrates. The other is the process of creating, provisioning and operating IT: the inner workings of the IT department.

IT process changes

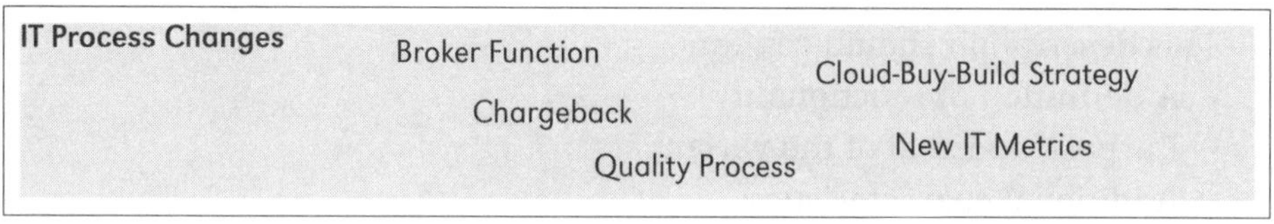

IT Process Changes		
Broker Function		Cloud-Buy-Build Strategy
Chargeback		
	Quality Process	New IT Metrics

Figure 9.5: IT process changes due to cloud computing

Including external cloud services in the corporate IT domain will have an impact on other dimensions of IT. Cloud may offer new or different functionality for the same process, the quality of the service may be different, or more practically, simple things like the way backups and restores are done could be entirely different. Also, for private clouds, there will be an impact on the IT processes.

You can initiate changes to prepare the IT process for cloud computing:

Embrace enterprise architecture in IT
Having enterprise architecture as a practice and as a process for aligning business and technology will only work if conforming to architectural principles is part of everyday life in the IT department. EA should be geared towards making the architecture guidance easy to digest and receptive to projects and other IT activities, but strong commitment is needed on the part of, for example, project managers and (senior) IT management.

For example, the infrastructure architecture methodology introduced in Chapter 6 should give you concrete tools to talk about the cloud from the infrastructure up, but it will only work if the people who actually work on infrastructure projects use it to guide their decisions.

Define and fulfill the cloud broker function

If the IT department wants to coordinate the journey to the cloud, it should at least function as a broker between business and end-users on the one hand and cloud service providers on the other hand (see Chapter 5). This much-discussed broker function is, on the one hand, very straightforward (simply match supply and demand) and, on the other hand, it may turn out to be the difference between winning and losing market share.

In essence, the broker function has an internal side, of knowing the demand and potential future demand, and it has an external side, of pro-actively scouting for possible services that can be relevant to the business. To start the broker function, all it takes is some time for people to initiate both sides: define expected demand and do a market scan of potential new services.

But once the number of services managed by the broker function starts growing, there will be additional demands on the broker: guaranteeing quality, continuity, reducing risk and watching for legal issues. If you use a broker-selected cloud service, you should be able to trust the parties who deliver services that may be business-critical or who store data that might be sensitive. This trust should be underpinned by proper legal contracts and service agreements. When setting up the broker function for the cloud, it is advisable to set up profiles of potential provider companies, containing criteria regarding financial and legal aspects, compliance, security, personnel, location, *etc*. These profiles can be used when including new services into the corporate set of solutions.

As a long-term goal, it may be useful to keep the concept of a corporate app store in mind: a self-provisioning portal where users can sign up for applications and services that are relevant to them. In this app store, you would present the complete portfolio of internal and external applications in a user-friendly way. Populating the app store would be the responsibility of the cloud broker.

Start using a service portfolio

To fulfill the role of broker well, a consistent, extensive and dynamically maintained service portfolio is indispensable. The IT department builds such a portfolio with internal and external services selected for their functional excellence, innovation, service excellence and cost characteristics. Managing this portfolio is a new IT capability that goes beyond traditional supplier management. To set up a portfolio, you make an inventory of business capabilities (see Chapter 6) and map them onto the services they need. This way, a good understanding can be obtained about the use of services, the way they are re-used or shared, and the importance of the services for the proper operation of business processes (service priority).

Define and describe services in a technologically agnostic manner, in order to provide a clear overview of the functionality, quality and features of the services that are being delivered by the IT department, regardless of the way they are realized. At the same time, these definitions provide the requirements that architects can use to select feasible solutions, determining whether valid cloud candidates exist or not. In their turn, architects can provide input for the description of services by providing pattern definitions that describe the functional appearance of solutions.

Become more specific in cost allocation

To implement a service portfolio, the cost per service is important information. Since internal IT will in some ways be competing with external providers, transparency about cost is essential. To enable a pay-per-use costing model, with the correct chargeback to the business, you need good insight into the metrics of IT. You need insight into the cost of operating IT, but also into how that cost is related to business relevant metrics such as transactions, products or users. Integration and orchestration costs of cloud services should be included in this model. Establish a cost allocation structure and charging model that covers all services, regardless of whether it is a cloud, a non-cloud or a partial cloud implementation, and you'll be ready for whatever cloud solution will be implemented along the way. Even if you will never adopt a true pay-per-use model in your organization, the insight is indispensable for proper financial control and justification.

Renew service management to guide delivery

When services are delivered by the cloud, it impacts both technical and operational processes (see chapters 5 and 6). The way a solution is realized changes, so this needs to be guided by architects. But what also changes is the responsibility for operational processes, their character or nature, and methods of service delivery and control. This means that service management is highly impacted by the cloud. Due to the dynamic nature of cloud computing, service portfolios become more dynamic and at the same time this leads to the existence of more underlying contracts. Services from different providers and of different types need to be presented to the business as a consistent set. Incident, problem and change management all need to be carried out in different forms, depending on the nature of the cloud services and the underlying service-level agreements. When renewing service management to make it ready for the cloud, at least the following processes should be changed to be capable of carrying out the task:

- Service portfolio management—as mentioned above, a service portfolio with standardized services defined in business terms. The necessary steps to establish this portfolio are already described above. The responsibility for keeping this portfolio up to date resides within service management.
- IT service continuity management—ensure service operation continuity. Distributed implementation of solutions (to different cloud providers) can put continuity at risk, if it is not guarded carefully.
- Help desk, incident and problem management—a governance structure and organization that are prepared for a high level of automation, the alignment of help desks with cloud providers, incident and problem management processes and agreements on problem management processes with cloud providers in order to be able to trace and solve problems (root cause analyses).
- Change and release management—mature and standardized processes that can be automated to support the rapid provisioning of cloud-related services.
- Availability and capacity management—a capacity forecasting model that can take into account the characteristics of cloud-related services.

Technology changes

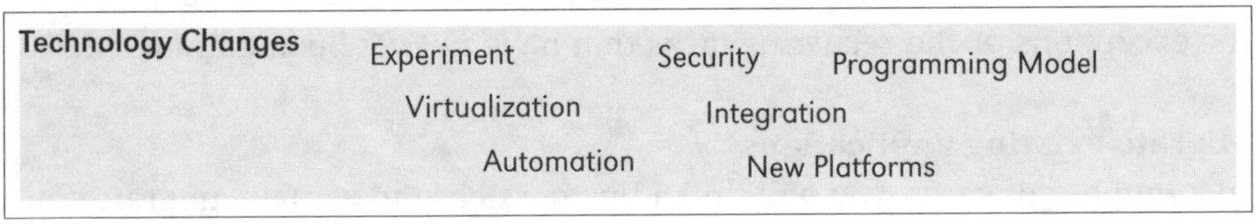

Technology Changes	Experiment	Security	Programming Model
	Virtualization	Integration	
	Automation	New Platforms	

Figure 9.6: Technology changes due to cloud computing

After talking about all the changes to process and business, one could almost forget that there is a technical impact as well. If you embrace cloud as an internal model, the technical focus might be on virtualization first. If you focus on using a public service, you might start with addressing security or integration. And there are some other concrete actions that lie ahead in the technology space:

Experiment!

Try some things out. Create a solution with the API's of public cloud. Self-provision some Amazon compute power and run an app on it. When experimenting, take the cloud concepts for a test drive and look in particular at the characteristics that will matter most:

- Security and performance.
- Managing and operations.
- New features, new possibilities.

Most developers love experimenting with the latest online platform, so if you give them half a chance they will come up with creative solutions. And if you can find a contained business-relevant experiment, involve the business in your experiments.

Virtualize your datacenter

It is one of the low-hanging fruits that most organizations have already grabbed: start a project to find redundant hardware and reduce the number of physical machines. This will bring down the cost and increase your agility right away. It has fairly limited business visibility, if you do it right, and it will help you prepare for the addition of external resources, too.

Automate manual IT processes

When the pressure on cost remains high, and competition from cloud service providers increases, the cost of basic IT operations needs to approach that of the external providers. The most important way to do this is to automate as much as possible in the IT operations domain. Look for the manual processes, the exceptions or the recurring tasks that have not yet been automated.

Migrate existing applications

In a number of cases, you will find a business case to actually migrate some existing applications to the cloud. If a cloud service is available that offers the functionality currently offered by the existing application, you would enter into a data-migration project. If no ready-made alternative is available, you can port the existing application to a cloud platform. In this case, a review of the application architecture is in order: how does the application handle threading, scaling, transactions, storage *etc*. Then select the cloud platform that fits the application best, and still conforms to the business case.

Get ready for integration

If you already have an SOA, you will probably have some sort of enterprise service bus. When adopting cloud computing, integration will become one of the core technical skills of the IT department. Providing a stable, mature integration platform that can scale to the demands that cloud may bring will be critical to the core function of IT. At least consider master data management, identity & permission management, policy management, workflow orchestration, messaging facilities and reliable network connectivity. If your integration approach is not yet perfect, this is the time to address it. It prevents the creation of a patchwork of unmanageable, incompatible platforms. Without a sound integration approach, anarchy and chaos stand waiting at the door bearing their gift of increased complexity, which will lead to reduced flexibility and higher costs.

9.5 Inside-Out or Outside-In?

Generally, adoption of cloud computing comes from two sides. One is the IT optimization path, looking to reduce cost and increase agility. The other is from the outside-in, where complete user-ready solutions are introduced because they address an urgent business need. The two different types of adoption can, to some extent, be combined.

Adopt cloud outside-in

The first approach is the simplest one in the beginning. It means that an organization eclectically picks services and apps from the (public) cloud that provide simple commodity or isolated niche services. Examples of commodities are email and teleconference services. Examples of niche services are human resource test tools or collaboration portals from the cloud. These applications can be acquired easily, mostly by subscription to a service. In many cases, all one needs is a web browser and a credit card. The functionality offered is often closely related to specific user groups who carry out specific tasks. However, integration of these applications with other applications is zero or close to zero. Although initial implementation is simple, lack of integration and possible issues regarding data security and legal obligations make this approach not suitable for all purposes. And, in the long run, a complex patchwork of disconnected applications and facilities made up with services from all corners of the cloud isn't exactly a tempting scenario for most organizations.

Adopt cloud inside-out

The second approach is much harder in the beginning, but seems to be more future-proof in the long run. With this approach, internal facilities are transformed into (private) cloud services by using virtualization techniques, service orchestration and integration facilities, automated management facilities, self-service portals and charging mechanisms, to name some important cloud ingredients. This requires a complete revision of the IT landscape, to become a landscape built upon the principles of service orientation. Once internal services are in place (including orchestration and integration facilities), external cloud services can be obtained and incorporated into the total set of IT services of an organization. These might be application platforms and storage facilities that extend beyond the firewalls of the organization's own data center, for disaster recovery, developing and testing or peak-load handling purposes. They might be external service routines that handle portions of data processing jobs in a real SOA fashion. This approach is thorough and only provides clear benefits further down the road. It might be hard to explain to business representatives and difficult to interest them. At a minimum, a concise set of principles and reference models is needed to support decision making.

If an IT department would ignore cloud altogether, the outside in approach would silently chip away at the core function of IT. Over time, less and less would be asked from the IT department, but at the same time integration and process integrity would probably suffer. A complete inside-out approach might feel very safe and robust, but can suffer from the same ills that ultimately gave SOA a bit of a bad reputation in the end: a lot of internal preparation that does not directly create new business opportunities. Cost saving is wonderful, and increasing agility is much desired, but nothing creates excitement like new business opportunities. That is why a combined approach would be ideal: aim for the biggest improvements internally while scouting the public cloud for new opportunities. Apply good architectural principles to whatever decision you make, and over time the two approaches will have reached the desired end state of a portfolio that consists of a mix of internal and external services, brokered by an internal broker function.

9.6 Learning More About Cloud & Understanding the Full Impact

Throughout the organization, more learning and exploration is probably in order to creating a better understanding of cloud computing and its full impact. There are many ways to do this, some of which were mentioned before. There are some other concrete actions you can initiate:

- Visit cloud computing events or training. There are many events that explain cloud and share best practices. CloudCamp is a so called "unconference" that comes recommended for enterprise architects and technical people (see http://cloudcamp.org).
- Get the legal team on board by initiating the discussion now. Help them explore the regulatory hurdles around cloud and find ways to overcome them.
- Do an IT or EA maturity assessment, to get third-party feedback on the strengths and weaknesses of your current IT or EA organization. Did you implement SOA? Is the EA process working well? Learn where you are in need of improvement before embracing the changes that come with cloud.
- Do a security scan, to find out if risk management, security policies and technologies are good enough to start thinking about integrating into a cloud ecosystem.
- Do a round of fact finding around the (im)possibilities of cloud computing. Visit the QA and testing teams, the people who operate existing applications. Their input and even objections can be very valuable to establish the impact cloud computing will have for you.

Many of the concepts are not new, and often it is the case of simply applying what we already know. The discussion about cloud gives you the opportunity to set some things straight where correction was sorely needed. Spreading knowledge of how IT could and should work is an important part of that: establish the ideal to initiate the journey towards it.

9.7 Cloud in Your Organization

Business Changes	Increase Tech-savvy	Business Technology Ecosystem Company
	Dynamic Partnering	
	Self-provision	
	Experiment New Budgeting	"Data as the new frontier"

Business ←→ IT Interaction Changes	Enterprise Architecture	
		Services Portfolio
	Evaluate Value	
	Business-IT Strategy	Innovation Committee

IT Process Changes	Broker Function	Cloud-Buy-Build Strategy
	Chargeback	New IT Metrics
	Quality Process	

Technology Changes	Experiment	Security Programming Model
	Virtualization	Integration
	Automation	New Platforms

Figure 9.7: Summary of changes due to cloud computing

Technology is the basis of cloud, but the changes span the organization. The priority and depth at which the different aspects will be executed will vary from place to place. In general, you'd adopt everything in the diagram roughly from left to right, allowing some experimentation and initial steps before starting the cloud initiative in earnest. And though your exact order of adoption might differ, there are of course interdependencies, for example between virtualization and chargeback, or between automation and self provisioning.

9.8 Living in the Cloud

In the end, cloud will follow the path of SOA: SOA is no longer in the public eye as an important theme, but it is still the leading model for designing distributed systems. Cloud is fast becoming simply "one more option" for IT, but its true value will be found by the companies that turn an IT trend into a business opportunity. Along the way, cloud will have pushed IT to a new level of professionalism, making it an organic part of the business at the same time. But its promises are not fulfilled without effort. It requires hard labor, coordination, collaboration and creativity, together with clear milestones and acknowledged and celebrated successes. The steps suggested do not stand alone, nor can they be taken separately. They are related to each other and need to be carried out in an iterative process that slowly incorporates processes, people and technology. Remember, it's not a migration, it's adopting a new paradigm, a journey. Choose your destination and pace. And then set sail, if you are not under sail already. Good luck!

About IBM

International Business Machines Corporation, abbreviated IBM, is a global technology and innovation company headquartered in Armonk, New York, and with locations in 170 countries. Utilizing its business consulting, technology and R&D expertise, IBM helps clients around the world become "smarter" as the planet becomes more digitally interconnected. That includes working with organizations and governments to build systems that improve traffic congestion, food safety, the availability of clean water, and the health and safety of populations. IBM invests more than \$6 billion a year in R&D, holding more patents than any other US company. IBM offers a wide range of infrastructure and consulting services; a broad portfolio of software for collaboration, predictive analytics and systems management; and the world's most advanced servers and supercomputers.

About Sogeti

Sogeti is a leading provider of professional technology services, specializing in Application Management, Infrastructure Management, High-Tech Engineering and Testing. Working closely with its clients, Sogeti enables them to leverage technological innovation and achieve maximum results. Sogeti brings together more than 20,000 professionals in 15 countries and is present in over 100 locations in Europe, the US and India. Sogeti is a wholly-owned subsidiary of Cap Gemini S.A., listed on the Paris Stock Exchange. For more information please visit www.sogeti.com.

About Sogeti and the cloud

Sogeti provides a set of cloud services based on a fully automated environment, with "triple play" solutions on site, near site, rightshore, matching your specific business needs, with appropriate service level agreements and billing models. We cover the entire spectrum of the ongoing transformation cycle generated by cloud computing, from consulting to operation. For more information please visit www.sogeti.com/cloud.

The People Who Contributed

This book could not have been created without the suggestions and feedback from many contributors. We would especially like to thank the following people for their time and insights, which helped shape this book and the interviews in it: Måns Adler, Mike Blake, Ben Gorter, Rob Keemink, Tony Kerrison, Johan Krebbers, Scott Orn, Paul Suijkerbuijk, Laurentiu Vasiliu, and Hennie Wesseling. Also, special thanks go to the many clients that we have worked with or that we have interviewed about their experiences with cloud computing. Tony Kontzer did wonderful work to create the case descriptions. Finally, we thank the IBM-Sogeti alliance team, which played a crucial role in making this book possible.

Below you will find the list of this book's authors and contributors. Feel free to contact them directly!

"Doing cloud without EA is like flying without air traffic control."

Martin van den Berg
Sogeti, The Netherlands

Martin van den Berg is Architecture Service Line Manager at Sogeti Nederland B.V. and an expert in the area of enterprise architecture. He has worked as lead architect in organizations like ABN AMRO, ING and Shell. Martin is one of the founders of DYA (Dynamic Architecture) and author of several books on enterprise architecture and SOA. Martin is chairman of the Architecture Section of the Dutch Computer Society and represents Sogeti in the Open Group. He has written many articles and presented papers at many conferences on EA and SOA.

http://nl.linkedin.com/in/mjbkvandenberg

"Cloud computing cannot be ignored. Business users are more and more in flavor of using cloud applications. As CIO, be the 'Cloud Implementation Officer'."

Jean-Michel Bertheaud
IBM, France

Jean-Michel is based in Paris. He has been the Executive IT Architect in charge of Sogeti World Wide for many years. His core responsabilities are to maintain, build and co-ordinate the global technical activities and relationships between Sogeti and IBM. Working closely with local IBM teams that support Sogeti, he is a trusted advisor to Sogeti, particularly to technical leaders and innovators on the global stage. Jean-Michel has been driving innovation and the development of innovative solutions using IBM components like "Innovation Jam" hosted in IBM's Dublin Cloud Computing Center in 2008, followed in 2009 by an internal collaborative tool project. In 2010, Jean-Michel has been the lead architect and IBM project director for the Sogeti Cloud Center in Paris.

http://www.linkedin.com/in/jmbertheaud

"Success with cloud requires strategy and architecture, not just more architects—rather, more strategy and architectural awareness."

Per Björkegren
Sogeti, Sweden

Per Björkegren has the roles of CTO and consultant within Sogeti Sweden. He spends most of his time on consulting, especially in the areas of IT strategy and enterprise architecture, but he also regularly presents seminars and speeches.

Sometimes Per dives deeper into solution architecture and design. Since 2004, three of his efforts have led to Microsoft .NET Awards. Even though Per hasn't been doing programming since the early 90's, he still ranks on Computer Sweden's list of the most important developers in the country. Most recently he was listed as #36.

Per is the founder and chairman of Swedish Enterprise Architecture Network, SWEAN, which today has about 600 members and is mainly administered on LinkedIn. He was also co-author of the book *SOA for Profit*.

http://se.linkedin.com/in/bjorkegren

"Every success and failure starts with the end user."

Rik den Boogert
Sogeti, The Netherlands

Rik den Boogert is Service Line Manager Implementation and is responsible for the development of Implementation Services within Sogeti Netherlands. Rik has gained experience over more than 30 years in the IT industry, covering many management and consultancy roles in numerous branches like utilities, finance, telecom and government. Nowadays he is more and more focused on the end user, since that is where success and failure starts. That is an obvious truth that is easily forgotten. This is also the case with cloud computing. It is Rik's mission to bring this thinking to the hearts and minds of the IT people.

http://nl.linkedin.com/pub/rik-boogert/3/693/50a

"How could we manage cumulonimbus without creating a storm?"

Flavien Boucher
Sogeti, France

Flavien Boucher is Senior Consultant and Global Lead IBM Cloud Collaboration. He is based in Washington DC, USA.

http://www.linkedin.com/pub/flavien-boucher/12/917/760

"Cloud computing is the biggest change in the IT industry in years. It's the first time that Business and Technology have been so close. For companies, the question is not when do they need to go in the cloud, but what will happen if they don't."

Bernard Huc
Sogeti, France

Bernard is a Certified Enterprise Architect with 30+ years of experience in IT. Bernard is working on the cloud computing services offered by Sogeti. Working in enterprise architecture for 15 years, Bernard has led the Global Architects Community of Capgemini Group where the day-to-day activities have been revolving around service-oriented architecture, business-IT alignment and cloud computing for a while. As part of this activity, Bernard has contributed to many innovation initiatives of the Capgemini group. Bernard is used to working in the international environment and has been involved in many international initiatives for customers around the world. Bernard is skilled in training and coaching people, and is often asked by the media to speak on IT trends.
Bernard is based in Grenoble, France.

http://www.linkedin.com/in/bernardhuc

"It's an architect's job to debunk the hype without missing opportunities. That applies to the cloud, for sure."

Daniël Jumelet
Sogeti, The Netherlands

Daniël is an experienced infrastructure and architecture consultant from The Netherlands. With a background in networking technology and information security, he developed an innovative infrastructure architecture methodology. He is the author of the book *DYA|Infrastructure, Architecture for the Foundations of IT* (Dutch) and has published several articles on the subject internationally.
Daniël advises and coaches several large organizations in the application of infrastructure architecture and practices it by directing complex infrastructure change processes. Next to his focus on architecture, he also has a keen interest in human sciences and philosophical issues, particularly regarding the interactions between people, society and technology.

"Making cloud work for an organization, and not just add complexity and risk to their IT, is the most exciting opportunity and challenge facing the CIO today."

Mark Kerr

IBM, United Kingdom

Mark Kerr is an IBM Executive IT Architect, working primarily with computer services industry clients and partners. He has been interested in the cloud since its early days, and believes it has the same potential to change the industry as the PC did in the 80's and the Internet did in the 90's. Mark is currently engaged in building a cloud services platform for a major IT service provider, and is also a member of IBM UK's cloud strategy team. He is an Open Group Distinguished IT Architect and Chartered IT Professional.

http://uk.linkedin.com/pub/mark-kerr/4/41b/820

"Cloud computing is a natural evolution of the IT environment that is here to stay, although it will keep on evolving as we see its strategic component rise before us. The forecast is: 'Cloudy, with a chance'."

Alfonso Lopez de Arenosa

Sogeti, Spain

Alfonso Lopez de Arenosa, Senior Manager at Sogeti Spain, is responsible for cloud sales on the IBM platform for Sogeti Europe. Alfonso has been in IT for more than 20 years, having covered every position in a datacenter, from being a console operator to being in charge of a datacenter, and having watched the evolution of the mainframe as part of the evolution of his own career. He has successfully managed the Sogeti-IBM relationship during the past 6 years, and is now taking the lead to develop cloud sales in Europe, with the goal of creating market awareness and helping customers to take the right steps into the cloud.

http://es.linkedin.com/pub/alfonso-lopez-de-arenosa/1/502/776

"Cloud is not really a revolution but rather an evolution, bringing several service provisioning and consumption capabilities together, leading to the dream of having IT available anywhere, at any time… while respecting work-life integration…"

Eric Michiels
IBM, Belgium

Eric Michiels is Client Technology Advisor in the financial services sector in Belgium. His role is to design solutions addressing business and IT challenges of banks, insurers and clearing houses. These solutions encompass cloud services, service-oriented architectures, and business process management. Working as an IT professional since 1986, Eric has acquired a broad experience in multiple industries, on several technical platforms and with many application architectures, while applying several development paradigms. Eric is Open Group Certified Distinguished Lead Architect and a TOGAF 9 Certified Professional. He is also IBM Liaison of the Belgian GSE Architecture Working Group and a fellow at Leuven University.

http://be.linkedin.com/pub/eric-michiels/0/513/818

"From a technology point of view cloud is an evolution, combining several developments of the past decade; from a business and users point of view it is a true revolution, changing the impact of IT on our lives forever."

Ron Moerman
Sogeti, The Netherlands

Ron Moerman is Technology Officer for Sogeti's Infrastructure Division in The Netherlands, and plays a leading role in developing the division's solutions and strategy. Drawing on more than 25 years of experience in IT, from mainframe to PC systems, Ron likes to discuss the possibilities of new technology, like cloud, for IT and business, helping customers develop the right strategy for their infrastructure. In the last 12 years he has developed several commercially successful solutions for Sogeti. A few years ago, he published a book on InFraMe® that covers an infrastructure project methodology, filling the gap between process and technology. Currently, Ron is one of the frontrunners on cloud topics within Sogeti Netherlands, helping customers and colleagues assess the limits and possibilities of cloud solutions.

http://nl.linkedin.com/in/ronmoerman

"Cloud computing should not be used as an excuse to forget everything about good IT practice and business fundamentals. They still apply!"

Brian Naylor
IBM, United Kingdom

Brian Naylor is the EMEA lead for cloud computing in the Cloud Engagement team within IBM Software Group. Responsible for being the catalyst for starting cloud projects with customers in Europe, Brian has 2-3 years of experience designing, implementing and enhancing private and public cloud solutions. With over 100+ customer engagements, Brian and the Cloud Engagement team have gained great insight into the reality of cloud computing in the business world.

http://uk.linkedin.com/in/banaylor

"To make sure that clouds do not just 'block the sun,' good insight in the required services and service levels from a business perspective is a prerequisite. Key to successful use of cloud services is to know why and how to use them."

Bert Noorman
Sogeti, The Netherlands

Bert Noorman is Service Line Manager at Sogeti Nederland B.V. In that role he is responsible for business development in the area of business processes and process management. He has broad experience: he combines business and IT aspects and works in multidisciplinary environments, as the integration of disciplines becomes more and more important. He is the author of several publications, including a book on quality assurance in projects.

http://nl.linkedin.com/pub/bert-noorman/3/532/b8

"As clouds in nature vary from simple to complex formations, so too in computing."

Liam Ó Móráin
Data Fonics, Germany

An engineer by training and an entrepreneur by vocation, Liam has extensive business experience, having run his own company, worked as a management consultant and served on the boards of several companies. He is a trusted advisor to several senior executives and a recognized thought leader on the future of the Internet. As a result of his many years working in the US and Europe, he has cultivated an impressive network of contacts on both sides of the Atlantic. He is currently working on a start-up which will employ cloud computing to provide real-time analysis of new feeds.

http://de.linkedin.com/in/liamomorain

"Calling it 'cloud' combined a bunch of trends into a coherent package that is a significant step forward for business technology."

Erik van Ommeren
Sogeti, USA

Erik is responsible for VINT, Sogeti's international research institute, in the USA. The research institute publishes and organizes events around trends such as open innovation, new media, Web 2.0, the commoditization of IT, IT governance, collaboration and cloud computing. Erik is an analyst with a broad background in IT and experience ranging from software development using many different technologies to enterprise architecture and executive management. Part of his time is spent advising organizations on transformation projects, architectural processes and innovation. Erik is also a trainer, speaker at seminars and author of several books and articles. Erik is based in Washington, DC.

http://www.linkedin.com/in/erikvanommeren

"I am using the cloud to create my collection of interesting architectural objects directly in a geomap in the cloud, so that I can use it as a local directory and guide anywhere, and without my wife's pressure to arrange it.
The most impressive thing about evolutions in a global context, including cloud, is that it is driven by its own ambition and cannot be predicted."

Paul Poelmans
Sogeti, Belgium/Luxembourg

Paul graduated as an architect and civil engineer where he was trained in combining creativity and technical realism in solutions meant for people. He is integrating these skills in his current job as Leader of Expertise in "innovation through Application Lifecycle Management and Architecture" to develop solutions for customers. Paul has worked as a consultant all over the world. He has trained people and presented on different topics, focusing on both technology and the impact of technology on the people who use it. He is combining his current job with the role of managing the global partnership between Oracle and Sogeti.

http://be.linkedin.com/in/paulpoelmans

"The cloud business model will change IT in a commodity for the business to use as tap water; turn it on and off when needed."

Ewald Roodenrijs
Sogeti, The Netherlands

Ewald is a member of the business development team within Sogeti Netherlands and the global lead of the Test Cloud within the Sogeti Group. As the global lead around the Sogeti Test Cloud he is responsible for the services around software testing and cloud computing services. He's also the co-author of the book *TMap NEXT®—BDTM*, a speaker at (international) conferences, an author of various national and international articles in expert magazines and has created various training courses.

http://nl.linkedin.com/in/ewaldroodenrijs

"As a child I was said to have 'my head in the clouds,' but now my feet are firmly on the ground so I can help others innovate in the cloud."

Pascal Sire
IBM, France

Pascal Sire is an innovation catalyst at IBM, teaming with strategic alliances and enabling global systems integrators to adopt innovative technologies and social networking. Previously, Pascal was a technical expert in new technologies at IBM. He was also an Internet entrepreneur before the dotcom bubble burst. He is an engineer and holds an Advanced Masters in Innovative Design (TRIZ expertise), and now extends his business interests to strategies for intellectual capital and innovation. Pascal is also a trainer, seminar facilitator and author of several articles on these matters. Pascal is based in Strasbourg (headquarters of the European Parliament).

http://www.viadeo.com/profile/00222h9y9ebk4km4

"Cloud will have an impact on how we perform business, how we do IT and how we go about our everyday lives. The question is no longer if or when, it's a question of now and how."

Jimmy Sterner
Sogeti, Sweden

Jimmy Sterner is a senior enterprise architect at Sogeti, Sweden. He has a broad background in IT business where he has been active in many fields such as system development, system design, business object modeling, process modeling, system architecture, project management, IT architecture and enterprise architecture.

Jimmy Sterner is TOGAF certified and has a Swedish IT-architect certificate. He has specific knowledge and interest in the fields of integration and information architecture. Throughout his career he's been working in the area between IT and business, with questions concerning the harmonic alignment and understanding between the two.

http://se.linkedin.com/pub/jimmy-sterner/1/472/93b

"Cloud computing is one of the most impactful transformations organizations will go through in the next decade, fundamentally changing the dialog, we see today, between Business and IT."

Sunil Talreja
Sogeti, USA

Sunil Talreja is the Vice President for Sogeti's Enterprise Solutions Consulting Practice in the USA, and plays a lead role in services innovation, industrialization and consultant enablement. Sunil has served 15 years with the Capgemini/Sogeti Group, during which he has advised clients on business and IT transformation leveraging information and technology capabilities, including analytics, service oriented architecture, convergence of media, mobile and mobility, and process automation to name a few. He specializes in the design and implementation of strategies and capabilities for organizations to proactively leverage emerging and impactful technologies for leapfrog business advantage.

http://www.linkedin.com/pub/sunil-talreja/1/7a3/81a

References

AWS (Amazon Web Services). 2009. Creating HIPAA-compliant medical data applications with AWS. White paper. http://aws.amazon.com/about-aws/whats-new/2009/04/06/whitepaper-hipaa/.

Alford, Ted and Gwen Morton. 2010. *The economics of cloud computing, addressing the benefits of infrastructure in the cloud*. Booz, Allen, Hamilton. http://www.boozallen.com/media/file/Economics-of-Cloud-Computing.pdf.

Ambrust, Michael, *et al*. 2009. *Above the clouds: a Berkeley view of cloud computing*. White paper. UC Berkeley Reliable Adaptive Distributed Systems Laboratory. http://radlab.cs.berkeley.edu/publication/285.

Anderson, Chris. 2006. *The long tail*. Random House.

Anderson, Chris. 2009B. The new new economy: more startups, fewer giants, infinite opportunity. *Wired*, 17-06. http://www.wired.com/culture/culturereviews/magazine/17-06/nep_essay##ixzz0uDkeR72d.

Anderson, Janna Quitney and Lee Rainie. 2010. The future of cloud computing. *The Future of the Internet*. Pew Research Center. http://www.pewInternet.org/~/media//Files/Reports/2010/PIP_Future_of_the_Internet_cloud_computing.pdf.

BBC Music. [undated]. http://www.bbc.co.uk/music. Accessed December 2010.

Berg, Martin van den, Norbert Bieberstein and Erik van Ommeren. 2007. *SOA for profit*. Sogeti.

Berg, Martin van den and Marlies van Steenbergen. 2006. *Building an enterprise architecture practice*. Springer.

Berners-Lee, Tim, James Hendler and Ora Lassila. 2001. The semantic web. *Scientific American*. May 17. http://www.scientificamerican.com/article.cfm?id=the-semantic-web.

Bias, Randy. 2010. Understanding cloud datacenter economies of scale. *Cloud Scaling*. http://cloudscaling.com/blog/cloud-computing/understanding-cloud-datacenter-economies-of-scale.

Bloem, Jaap et al. 2009. *Me the media: rise of the conversation society*. Uitgeverij Kleine Uil. http://www.methemedia.com.

Blumauer, Andreas. 2009A. Interview with Chris Bizer. *Semantic Web Company*. April 17. http://www.semantic-web.at/1.36.resource.278.chris-bizer-x22-within-the-corporate-market-there-is-interest-in-using-linked-data-as-a-li.htm.

Blumauer, Andreas. 2009B. BBC music relaunch: linked data goes business? *Semantic Web Company*. April 8. http://blog.semantic-web.at/2009/04/08/bbc-music-relaunch-linked-data-goes-business.

Boulton, Clint. 2010. IBM preps for cloud computing war vs. Google, Microsoft in 2010. *E-week* blog 12-21. http://www.eweek.com/c/a/Cloud-Computing/IBM-Preps-For-Cloud-Computing-War-Vs-Google-Microsoft-in-2010-634462/.

Bradshaw, Mike. 2010. Testimony before the House Committee on Oversight and Government Reform, hearing on cloud computing: benefits and risks of moving Federal IT into the cloud. July 1. http://googlepublicpolicy.blogspot.com/2010/07/bringing-federal-it-into-cloud.html.

Bughin, Jacques, *et al*. 2010. Clouds, big data and smart assets: ten tech-enabled trends to watch. *McKinsey Quarterly*. August. http://www.mckinseyquarterly.com/High_Tech/Clouds_big_data_and_smart_assets_Ten_tech-enabled_business_trends_to_watch_2647.

CIA (Central Intelligence Agency). [undated]. *The world factbook*. https://www.cia.gov/library/publications/the-world-factbook. Accessed December 2010.

Cameron, Bobby. 2009. *BT changes IT's operating model*. Forrester Research.

Cameron, Bobby. 2010. *Put Your Emerging-Technology Strategy Into A Business Context — Globalization, BT Sourcing Strategies, And Digital Business Networks Define The Strategy*. Forrester Research.

Carr, Nicholas. 2009. *The big switch: rewiring the world, from Edison to Google*. W.W. Norton & Co.

Cast Iron. 2010. IBM acquires Cast Iron Systems. Press release. May. http://www.castiron.com/ibm.

Cisco. 2010. Visual Networking Index Global Mobile Data Traffic Forecast, 2009-2014. VNI forecast widget. http://ciscovni.com/vni_forecast/wizard.html.

The Corporate Executive Board Company. 2010. Executive summary. *The future of corporate IT*. http://www.executiveboard.com/it/pdf/The_Future_of_Corporate_IT.pdf.

Cyganiak, Richard, and Anja Jentzsch. 2010. Linking open data cloud diagram. Updated 2010. http://richard.cyganiak.de/2007/10/lod.

Data-Gov-A. [undated]. United States Government. http://www.data.gov. Accessed December 2010.

DBpedia. [undated]. http://dbpedia.org/About. Accessed December 2010.

DERI (Digital Enterprise Research Institute) International. [undated]. http://www.deri.org. Accessed December 2010.

DMTF (Distributed Management Task Force). 2010. Cloud management standards. http://dmtf.org/standards/cloud.

Dubie, Denise. 2010. Microsoft's Ballmer: 'For the cloud, we're all in'. *Network World*. March 4. http://www.networkworld.com/news/2010/030410-microsoft-ballmer-cloud.html.

Economist. 2008. Where the cloud meets the ground. *The Economist*. October 23. http://www.economist.com/research/articlesbysubject/displaystory.cfm?subjectid=348981&story_id=E1_TNQTTJND.

Espiner, Tom. 2009. G cloud will have an app store. *ZDnet UK*. December 3. http://www.zdnet.co.uk/news/it-strategy/2009/12/03/g-cloud-will-have-an-app-store-39920920/.

Ferguson, Tim. 2009. BBC taps Web 3.0 for new music site. *Business Week*. April 7. http://www.businessweek.com/globalbiz/content/apr2009/gb2009047_713777.htm.

Flyontime. 2010. Airport statistics. http://flyontime.us/statistics/airports/percentcancelleddepartures.

Gartner. 2009. Gartner says worldwide CRM market grew 12.5 percent in 2008. Press Release. July 15. http://www.gartner.com/it/page.jsp?id=1074615.

Gross, Grant. 2010. Lawmakers question the security of cloud computing. *ComputerWorld*. July 1. http://www.computerworld.com/s/article/print/9178793/Lawmakers_question_the_security_of_cloud_computing.

Hadoop. [undated]. http://hadoop.apache.org. Accessed December 2010.

Harley, Brian, Philip Nolan, Liam Ó Móráin and Mark Leyden. 2009. The semantic web: legal challenges. Society for Computers & Law. Aug/Sept, 20:3. http://www.scl.org/site.aspx?i=ed12655.

Hawke, Sandro. 2010. Introduction to linked data. Cambridge Semantic Web Gathering. June 8.

Hessler, Pierre. [undated]. TechnoVision. http://www.capgemini.com/services-and-solutions/technology/technovision/overview/. Accessed December 2010.

Higginbotham, Stacey. 2010. The origins of Amazon's cloud computing. *GigaOM* blog. June 18. http://gigaom.com/2010/06/18/the-origins-of-amazons-cloud-computing/.

IBM Smart Business. 2010. Dispelling the vapour around cloud computing. White paper. January. Index at http://www.ibm.com/ibm/cloud/resources.html#5. Paper at ftp://ftp.software.ibm.com/common/ssi/sa/wh/n/ciw03062usen/CIW03062USEN.PDF.

ITIL (IT Infrastructure Library). [undated]. Welcome to ITIL. http://www.itil-officialsite.com/home/home.asp. Accessed December 2010.

Jentzsch, Anja, *et al.* 2009. Linking open drug data. http://triplify.org/files/challenge_2009/LODD.pdf.

Kotler, Philip and John A. Caslione. 2009. *Chaotics: the business of managing and marketing in the age of turbulence*. Amacom Publishing.

Leake, Jonathan and Richard Woods. 2009. Revealed, the environmental impact of Google searches. *The Times*. http://technology.timesonline.co.uk/tol/news/tech_and_web/article5489134.ece.

Li Ding and Jim Hendler. 2009. Data-gov-cloud. Rensselauer Polytechnic Institute. http://data-gov.tw.rpi.edu/wiki/File:Data-gov-cloud-200910.png.

Linked Data. 2010. Index of 2010 talks. http://www.w3.org/2010/Talks/0608-linked-data/.

Linthicum, David. 2010. Determining the real value of cloud computing. *Intelligent enterprise* blog, August 4. http://intelligent-enterprise.informationweek.com/blog/archives/2010/08/determining_the.html.

Longbottom, Clive. 2008. Obstacles to cloud computing. *Information management.* November 5. http://www.information-management.com/news/10002177-1.html.

Luijpers, Joost. 2009. Project Start Architecture. White paper. http://eng.dya.info/ Images/White_paper_Project_Start_Architecture_V1%200_tcm14-53669.pdf.

Maitland, Jo. 2009. Cloud computing, why now. *Tech Target IT Agenda.* August 20. http:// itagenda.blogs.techtarget.com/2009/08/20/cloud-computing-why-now/.

Mangum, Ynema. 2009. The cloud economy: part 3. Sun Microsystems blog. April 6. http://blogs.sun.com/humancloud/entry/the_cloud_economy_part_3.

Matzke, Pascal. 2010. *Making sense of cloud computing.* Forrester Research.

McCarthy, John and Pascal Matzke. 2010. *The coming upheaval in tech services.* Forrester Research.

Meeker, Mary, *et al.* 2010. Connectivity = cloud computing. *Internet trends.* Morgan Stanley. June 7. http://www.morganstanley.com/institutional/techresearch/pdfs/ MS_Internet_Trends_060710.pdf.

Miller, Michael. 2010. Cisco: Internet moves 21 exabytes per month. *PCMag.com.* March 25. http://www.pcmag.com/article2/0,2817,2361820,00.asp.

Mongo. [undated]. http://www.mongodb.org. Accessed December 2010.

Noorman, Bert. 2006. Pronto®-BPM approach. Sogeti white paper. http://pronto.sogeti. nl/Home/index.jsp [Dutch], http://pronto.sogeti.nl/Images/White%20Paper%20 Pronto%20vs%201.0%20%20%20%20English%20Version%20-%20september%202009_ tcm360-54961.pdf [English].

The Open Group. [undated]. Cloud computing work group. https://www.opengroup. org/. Accessed December 2010.

The Open Group. 2009. *TOGAF™ Version 9.* Van Haren Publishing.

Pohle, George, Peter Korsten and Shanker Ramamurthy. 2005. *Component business models: making specialization real.* IBM Institute for Business Value. http://www- 935.ibm.com/services/us/imc/pdf/g510-6163-component-business-models.pdf.

Potter, Kurt. 2010. *Chargeback methods that will change IT competitiveness and effectiveness.* Gartner.

Prusak, Laurence. [undated]. http://www.laurenceprusak.com. Accessed December 2010.

Ried, Stefan. 2009. SAP and cloud computing: two strangers meet. Blog. July 7. http:// www.stefan-ried.de/2009/07/07/sap-and-cloud-computing/.

Ried, Stefan, Holger Kisker and Pascal Matzke. 2010. *The evolution of cloud computing markets.* Forrester Research.

Rightscale. [undated]. *Cloud computing management platform.* http://www.rightscale. com/index.php. Accessed December 2010.

RisknCompliance Consulting Group. 2010. Let's talk some "real" insider threat numbers—How can Access Governance and SIEM be useful as effective safeguards? September 15. http://rnc2.com/information-risk/accessgovernance- siem-effective-safeguards-against-insider-threats/.

Schadler, Ted. 2008. *Talking to your CFO about cloud computing*. Forrester Research.

Scott, Jeff. 2010. *IT capability maps help CIOs manage IT like a business*. Forrester Research.

Semantic Universe. 2010. Semantic technology conference. San Francisco. http://semtech2010.semanticuniverse.com.

Sheehan, Michael. 2009. "10 obstacles to cloud computing" by UC Berkeley and how GoGrid hurdles them. *GoGrid* blog. February 19. http://blog.gogrid.com/2009/02/19/10-obstacles-to-cloud-computing-by-uc-berkeley-how-gogrid-hurdles-them/.

Shread, Paul. 2010. Investors look for good news for Salesforce.com. *ECRMGuide.com* blog. August 17. http://www.ecrmguide.com/article.php/3899026/Investors-Look-for-Good-News-from-Salesforcecom.htm.

Skilton, Mark, *et al.* 2010. Building return on investment from cloud computing. White paper, Cloud Computing Working Group, The Open Group. http://www.opengroup.org/cloud/whitepapers/ccroi/index.htm.

Soat, John. 2010. SaaS strategy: what upper management wants to know. *Information Week*. Posted to Cloud Computing Zone by Onuora Amobi. http://www.cloudcomputingzone.com/2010/05/16/saas-strategy-what-upper-management-wants-to-know/.

Sogeti. [undated]. *DYA infrastructure repository*. http://dya-knowledge.sogeti.nl. Accessed December 2010.

Symons, Craig. 2009. *Best practices in IT financial management*. Forrester Research.

W3C, HCLSIG (Semantic Web for Health Care and Life Sciences Interest Group). 2010. Linking open drug data. http://esw.w3.org/HCLSIG/LODD.

W3C, SWEO (Semantic Web Outreach and Education Interest Group). 2010. Community project: linking open data. http://esw.w3.org/SweoIG/TaskForces/CommunityProjects/LinkingOpenData.

Wagter, Roel, *et al.* 2005. *Dynamic enterprise architecture: how to make it work*. Wiley.

Weiss, Chris. 2010. *Apple launches the Mac App Store*. http://gadgetcrave.com/apple-launches-the-mac-app-store/8683/.

Widder, Oliver. 2010. How to be a tough CIO. *Geek and Poke*. http://geekandpoke.typepad.com/geekandpoke/2010/02/how-to-be-a-tough-cio.html.

Wikipedia. [undated]. DBpedia. http://en.wikipedia.org/wiki/Dbpedia. Accessed December 2010.

Wikipedia. [undated]. Metcalfe's law. http://en.wikipedia.org/wiki/Metcalfe%27s_law. Accessed December 2010.

Woods, Dan. 2010. Marketing technologies bypass IT. http://www.forbes.com/2010/08/09/salesforce-jigsaw-marketo-technology-cio-network-marketing.html.

Index

RightScale 80